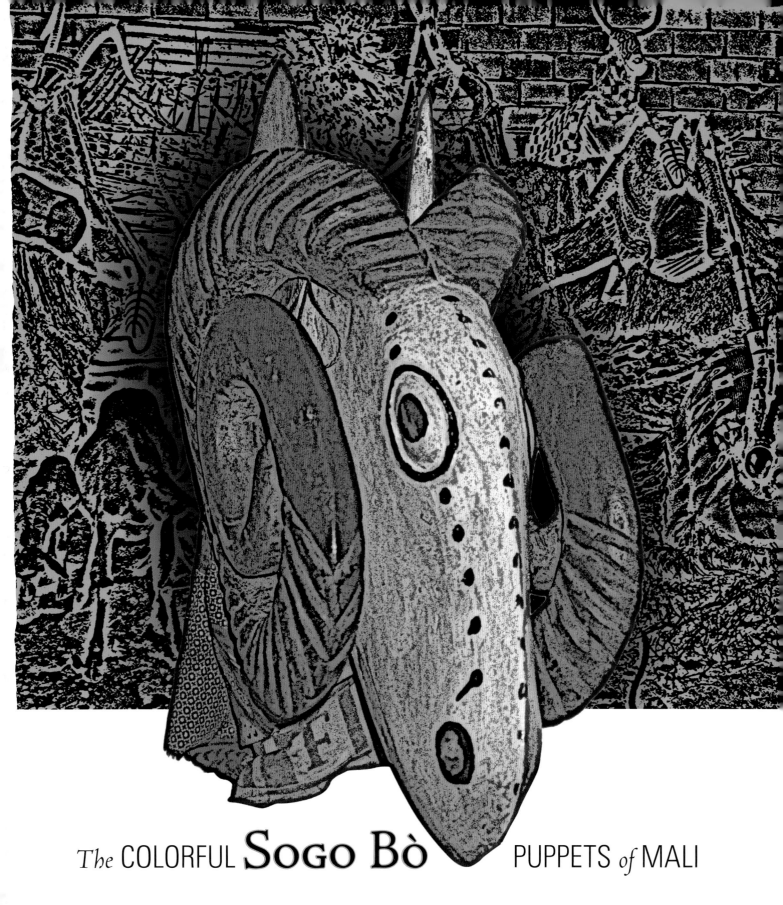

The COLORFUL **Sogo Bò** PUPPETS *of* MALI

MARY SUE ROSEN AND PAUL PETER ROSEN

Schiffer Publishing Ltd®

4880 Lower Valley Road • Atglen, PA 19310

Schiffer Books are available at special discounts for bulk purchases for sales promotions or premiums. Special editions, including personalized covers, corporate imprints, and excerpts can be created in large quantities for special needs. For more information contact the publisher:

Published by Schiffer Publishing Ltd.
4880 Lower Valley Road
Atglen, PA 19310
Phone: (610) 593-1777; Fax: (610) 593-2002
E-mail: Info@schifferbooks.com

For the largest selection of fine reference books on this and related subjects, please visit our website at www.schifferbooks.com
We are always looking for people to write books on new and related subjects. If you have an idea for a book, please contact us at proposals@schifferbooks.com

This book may be purchased from the publisher.
Please try your bookstore first.
You may write for a free catalog.

In Europe, Schiffer books
are distributed by
Bushwood Books
6 Marksbury Ave.
Kew Gardens
Surrey TW9 4JF England
Phone: 44 (0) 20 8392 8585
Fax: 44 (0) 20 8392 9876
E-mail: info@bushwoodbooks.co.uk
Website: www.bushwoodbooks.co.uk

Copyright © 2012 by Mary Sue Rosen and Paul Peter Rosen
Library of Congress Control Number: 2012931884

Designed by RoS
Type set in Adobe Jenson/Zurich BT

ISBN: 978-0-7643-4065-9
Printed in China

"*Whenever* someone endows an inanimate object with life force and casts it in a scenario, a puppet is born."

—Eileen Blumenthal, *Puppetry: A World History*

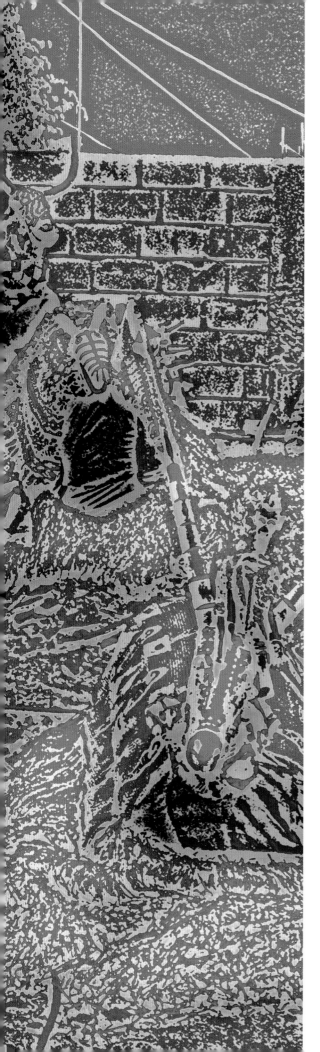

CONTENTS

PREFACE

Our passion for African art began with the purchase of occasional sculptures and masks found at street fairs in New York City. Some of these "treasures" are still with us as reminders of the early phase of this journey. Through reading we became entranced by African metalwork and the role that iron, copper, and brass objects used for adornment, currency and bride wealth played in the culture, history and art of Africa. Many of these patiently collected artful and functional creations were assembled for display in the first exhibition from our collection titled "Forms Transformed: An Exploration of African Metalwork" in January 2003 at The Pen and Brush Gallery in New York. The exhibition illustrated the inventive transformation of natural and utilitarian forms found in the extraordinary spectrum of African metal currency. Also on display were many of the traditional tools still used by blacksmiths we observed at work in the metal recycling market in Bamako, Mali, in 2003 and 2008 .

Textiles are also a traditional form of African currency. During a visit to Mali in 2003, sponsored by Drew University, we had an opportunity to observe a Boso weaver working in a village along the Niger River. A stunning blanket purchased from this skilled craftsman was the start of what has grown into a substantial collection of diverse, predominantly West African handwoven textiles. To learn more about this fine craft and to see weavers at work, we read extensively on the subject and made three trips to Ghana and Togo, most recently in March 2007. One of the highly treasured textiles acquired during these visits is a man's adinkra cloth made for us by Samuel Evans in the village of Ntonso. We watched this amazing artist deftly imprint a white cotton textile using stamps with adinkra symbols finely carved on pieces of calabash that he dipped into a pot of black ink made from the bark of the Badie tree and iron slag simmering over a charcoal fire.

Textiles were an important component of our 2004 Pen and Brush gallery exhibit, titled "Texture and Form: The Art of African Personal Objects," and our 2005 exhibition, "Puppets, Pottery and Textiles: African Traditions." In September 2006, we mounted an exhibition entirely devoted to African textiles entitled "Textile Arts from Sub-Saharan Africa."

Our interest in African puppet forms, and specifically Malian puppets, derives in large part from the fact that their creation and use in performance encompasses many genres of art: carving, blacksmithing, weaving, story telling and social commentary, poetry, singing, dancing, mime, and music. A community of hands is at work in bringing a Malian puppet to life, and a variety of materials is used in this process. Cloth that adorns a puppet often was used as clothing or in rituals. In a small way, this is a form of recycling. As we witnessed first hand, almost nothing is wasted in Africa. Materials of all kinds are reused and thereby gain new life.

On the aesthetic level, we are attracted to Malian puppets because of their vibrant colors and the expressiveness achieved by movement through articulation. These attributes contrast sharply with most of the monochromatic, wooden sculptural objects in our collection that are not articulated and are largely dark brown or black with sparse elements of applied pigment or colored bead work. It is this affinity for color that also attracted us to African textiles. Even out of the role for which they were created, when compared to their brown sculptural counterparts, we find that painted *Sogo bò* masks, puppets and puppet masquerades have a vibrancy that foretells the vitality we found them to embody in performance.

Malian puppets have a rich and evolving tradition as a vehicle for connecting entertainment to cultural, political, and historical aspects of community life. The inclusiveness of these performances links performers and audience in a common experience, wherein members of the community may themselves become participants. Honor is given to the past and lessons are reinforced for the present through these visually dramatic, colorful, musical and entertaining communal events. As collectors, it was essential for us to witness puppets in actual performances with music, song, and dance to further our understanding of this art form. It is our hope that the Malian masks and puppets illustrated in this volume will be appreciated not only as interesting, colorful, and expressive forms of art but also as manifestations of the enduring cultural heritage of Mali.

Despite our best efforts and good intentions as collectors and amateur students of the *Sogo bò* theatre tradition, it is possible that an unintended error may appear in the text or some point deemed to be important by others may have been incompletely addressed or omitted. These or any other defects that may appear in this book are solely the responsibility of the authors.

ACKNOWLEDGMENTS

Dr. Mary Jo Arnoldi, Curator Africa, Department of Anthropology at the Smithsonian Institution in Washington, D.C., is gratefully acknowledged for sharing her vast first-hand knowledge of Malian puppet traditions based on considerable field experience. Her extensive academic research and publications continue to inspire and inform our collection. It was a great honor to have Dr. Arnoldi curate the 2009 exhibition of masks and puppets from this collection at the SMA Fathers Museum of African Art in Tenafly, New Jersey, and to benefit from her authoritative contributions—including the documentation of the masks and puppets in that exhibition that are illustrated in this volume.

In 2010, we were invited to bring the exhibition of Malian puppets to the Free Library of Philadelphia, in Pennsylvania. Sincere thanks are extended to Siobhan Reardon, President and Chief Executive Officer of the Free Library, for her support and encouragement. Also in 2010, a selection of the masks and puppets was exhibited at the University of Memphis in Tennessee, and other puppets were displayed at the Please Touch Museum for children in Philadelphia.

We are very much indebted to Patricia Kuharic for her thoughtful, patient and essential contribution in preparing our photographs of the puppets, masks, and puppet performances for publication in this book. Pat has done a masterful job bringing these photographs to life.

We offer a special thanks to Yaya Coulibaly, with sincere appreciation for his warm and generous hospitality in hosting our 2008 visit to his home and allowing us the freedom to take photographs of his colleagues and atelier. At that time, we were able to bring him pictures of his youngest son, taken during our visit in 2003. In some small measure, we hope that this book conveys the spirit of this inspired, inventive artist and gifted teacher. Yaya Coulibaly is a treasure for the nation of Mali and, with the Sogolon Puppet Troupe that he founded, an international ambassador for the extraordinary creative arts and puppet tradition of Mali.

Our thanks also go to our African friends from Mali, especially Ousmane Camara for his friendship and guidance as well as to Moussa Diane, Mohamed Berete, Fafre Camara, and Yaya Traore. We gratefully acknowledge Samuel Sidibé, Director of the Musée National du Mali, who graciously took time from his busy schedule to speak with us about Malian puppetry during our 2008 visit. The Musée National is a sparkling jewel in West Africa and a shining credit to Mr. Sidibé's obvious commitment to and enthusiasm for the traditional and contemporary arts of Mali.

Several books listed in the Bibliography have been invaluable resources. Information about the history of puppetry can be found in *Puppetry: A World History* by Eileen Blumenthal and *Emotions in Motion* by Esther Dagan. Excellent discussions of puppetry throughout West Africa appear in the aforementioned volumes as well as in *Marionnettes et Masques au Coeur du Theatre Africain* by Olenka Darkowska-Nidzgorski and Denis Nidzgorski. Descriptions of Malian masks and puppets and discussions of their use in *Sogo bò* theater can be found in *Playing With Time* by Mary Jo Arnoldi, the essay "Masques et Marionnettes du Mali" by Amaëlle Favreau in *Marionnettes du Mali*, Werewere-Liking's *Marionnettes du Mali,* and *Sogo Bò. La Fête des Masques Bamanan* by Elisabeth den Otter and Mamadou Keita. Some of the masks, puppets, and puppet masquerades that we photographed in performance in 2008 are also illustrated and described in the latter volume.

INTRODUCTION

The English words "puppet," "poppet," "puppy," and "pupil" are derived from the Latin word *pupa*, meaning a doll or little girl. The word *pupa* itself was adopted to mean the larval form of an insect and applied in the word "pupil" to mean an undeveloped person. The origin of the word "puppet" is from the French word for a doll, *poupée*, through the early English form "poppet." At one time, the French word *poupée* also referred to a small dog, giving rise to "puppy" in English.

Puppetry is a form of performance art or theatre witnessed by an audience, in which one or more characters representing beings, inanimate objects or concepts are manipulated by independent operators, who may be visible or hidden from view. The vehicle for presenting the character in puppetry theatre is the "puppet," a performance object whose movement is completely controlled by an outside force. The manipulator of a puppet is the "puppeteer." The word "puppet" can also be an adjective, as for example in "puppet government," a reference to a political institution that appears to act independently when its actions are actually controlled by an external power. A puppet derives its vitality from its form and actions, the totality of the performance (including spoken words) and songs, as well as from the imagination of the audience. The variety of puppet forms and subjects that they can represent is almost infinite.

The special appeal of puppets derives from their nature as inanimate objects that are brought to life by the actions of an external force, the puppeteer. Motion, representation of a character, simplification, distortion, and exaggeration are properties of puppets that contribute to their success in making an emotional and intellectual connection with audiences of all ages. Serving as symbols or metaphors, puppets can be effective tools for education through entertainment or simply a source of entertainment.

In common with other forms of theatre, puppets act to transform emotions and concepts into movement and what appears to be imaginary into reality. In many cultures, puppets serve as a vehicle for communicating between the visible world people inhabit and the invisible, supernatural and spiritual realm. The operator is endowed with godlike power through the use of illusion to represent the strengths and weaknesses of the human condition as well as the mysteries and wonders of the natural world. Puppets often appear to be controlled by spiritual forces that allow them to express opinions or to act in ways that might not otherwise be humanly possible or socially acceptable. Their authoritative and sometimes playful voice permits them to criticize or reinforce patterns of behavior in the community. It is likely that the earliest forms of puppet theatre had a predominantly ritual function that later evolved into primarily secular performances intended mainly for celebration and entertainment. However, puppetry has always retained its inherently mystical character, and it often combines ritual, educational, and entertainment roles.

Although it is a strong, evocative art form in its own right, the power of puppetry is multiplied when it becomes part of a multimedia spectacle through the participation of one or more other performance modalities, such as song, narration, music or dance. The effect is further enhanced when formal barriers between the audience and performers, such as a stage and fixed seating for spectators, are omitted. All of these ancillary attributes are found in the Malian mask and puppet theatre tradition.

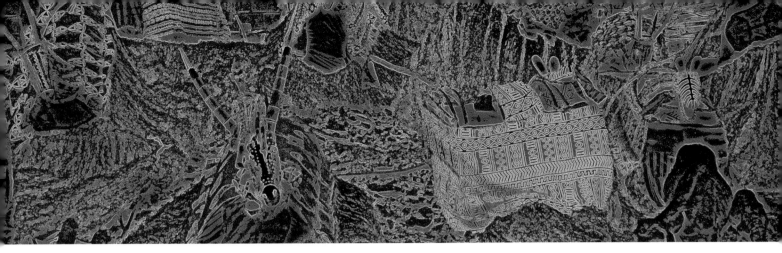

Masks are an integral part of the traditional Malian theatre performance repertory and, as discussed below, one source of Malian puppetry is probably rooted historically in the ritual use of masks and statues. Although they rarely appear in the same performance sequence as puppets, masked human figures that represent stereotypical persons, animals, spirits or mythical figures are such an important part of the theatre described in this book that they cannot be separated from the whole. Masks and puppets are performance objects that have similar freedom from reality that is derived from the power of transformation. After observing these performances, as well as speaking with local onlookers and with puppeteers, it became apparent that the masked performer could be viewed as a form of body puppet identified by a mask and costume that is inhabited by a hidden operator. As is the case with virtually all books on the subject of Malian puppetry, this volume distinguishes between masks and puppets as physical objects but presents them as parts of a single theatrical tradition.

In Malian *Sogo bò* theatre, it is essential that the puppeteer and the masked performer not be visible to the audience and that the spectators not see the performers as they assume the guises of the characters they are to become. As the animator of a puppet or mask, the puppeteer or masker is endowed with the secrets and spirit of the character. It is a role with mystical attributes that has been likened to returning to the womb and a responsibility that can only be assumed by an initiate. The sequences performed by masks complement those of the hidden performers who operate inanimate puppets.

The multimedia concept of Malian puppet theatre is consistent with the centuries-old, widespread tradition of integrating inanimate objects in the form of masks, statues, or puppets set in motion by human operators into theatrical performances that employ human actors. A spectacular, contemporary example of puppets appearing in a multimedia performance is the use of life-sized equine puppets manipulated by multiple operators as well as individually operated crows and a goose created by the South African Handspring Puppet Company for the play, *War Horse*, that was performed at the National and New London Theatres in London and the Vivian Beaumont Theatre in New York between 2007 and 2011. It is noteworthy that Basil Jones, co-founder of the Handspring Puppet Company with Adrian Kohler and two other graduates of the Michaelis School of Fine Art in Cape Town, was an "admirer" of Malian puppets. In an interview, Jones commented that, "the museum where I worked had acquired a small collection of these (Malian) puppets and I was curating them, so I came to respect this tradition and to be curious about puppetry as an African tradition that had nothing to do with the rest of the world." Around the same time, Kohler acquired a Bambara puppet from a Cape Town gallery.

Years after Jones and Kohler first became acquainted with the Malian puppet tradition, Yaya Coulibaly, the master Malian puppet maker and founder of the Sogolon Puppet Troupe, joined them in creating *Tall Horse*, a play based on the story of a giraffe sent in 1826 by the Sultan of Egypt as a gift to the King of France, Charles X. Yaya Coulibaly and the Handspring Company also collaborated in a show at the Irma Stern Museum in Cape Town, titled *Patrimony: An Exhibition of Malian Puppets,* and a 2006 New York World Financial Center exhibition hosted by The Museum for African Art in New York, titled *At Arm's Length: The Art of African Puppetry,* where many puppets from both organizations were displayed. Additional information about Yaya Coulibaly can be found in Chapter Four.

THE SHADOWY ORIGINS OF PUPPETRY:

a hypothesis

As the earliest humans roamed the land on sunny days and moonlit nights, they must have seen their shadows. With the acquisition of fire, shadows would also have been vividly present on the walls of caves and later in man-made habitations. It is reasonable to speculate that our ancestors would have recognized that the shadows mimed their movements. They would also have observed that the shapes of the shadows varied as the position of the person changed and that the speed and direction of movement was always controlled by the person who was the source of the shadow. Properties of shadows, such as the way they change in size and shape as one approaches or moves away from the surface on which they are cast, or the fact that shadows could be made to move in different directions, must have been mysterious phenomena to our earliest ancestors.

It would also have been apparent that shadows were cast by animals, and it surely must have been a source of wonder to see the shadow of a large bird moving across the ground on a clear, moonlit night or a sunny day. Our ancestors would also have seen shadows cast by inanimate objects such as rocks, trees, bushes, and even utilitarian things in their habitation such as spears, clubs, and animal skins. It would not have been a great leap to realize that the shadow cast on a wall by an inanimate object such as a stick or club could be made to move when held by a person. From these observations would come the realization that the shadows created by individuals alone, or by people having objects in their hands or attached to their bodies, could entertain and influence an audience. Thus, the shadow puppet would have been born. Perhaps the earliest creators of shadow puppets learned to expand their repertoire by creating objects to hold or covering themselves in ways that produced shadow images with recognizable forms such as animals. The mysterious nature of the event would have been enhanced when the unseen operator was positioned behind the audience between the light source and the surface on which the shadow was projected. The magical experience might have been more effective if the shadows were accompanied by sounds produced by the operator or an assistant. Eventually, the mystical and spiritual power of the shadow would be transferred to its physical source, leading to the birth of the puppet, puppeteer and puppetry theatre. Shadow puppetry remains an art form that is still widely practiced today. Once puppetry came out of the shadows, so to speak, the field was wide open to create the vast range of expressive costumes, masks, rod figures, and articulated characters that have animated puppetry for centuries throughout the world.

A SHORT HISTORY OF PUPPETRY

The foregoing hypothetical description of the origin of puppetry from shadows may be reasonable, but it is entirely speculative. The precise origin or source of puppetry will probably never be known. At best, it is possible to note the earliest available textual references to puppets and puppetry, the oldest images purported to show puppets, and doll-like objects excavated at archaeological sites that may have been used as puppets. This chapter is intended to provide a very brief overview of the history of puppets and puppetry as a background to the detailed discussion of Malian puppetry. More comprehensive information can be found in books listed in the Bibliography, especially *Puppetry: A World History* by Eileen Blumenthal.

The available fragmentary evidence suggests that puppetry probably arose independently in disparate parts of the globe to serve a basic need common to humanity. In non-literate societies, puppets were an important means of communication, and they continue to have this role today. The limited historical documentation that exists for puppetry is not unexpected because of the perishable nature of puppets as well as the essentially verbal and visual character of the art form.

Terracotta figures with separate heads and limbs, dating from around 2400 B.C.E., that might have been used as puppets were found in excavations in the Indus Valley in present-day Pakistan. A "walking" statue of a god, identified in an Egyptian hieroglyphic inscription from 2000 B.C.E., may be a puppet. Articulated figures have also been found in Pharaonic tombs from the same era. A fifth century B.C.E. description of puppets carried by Egyptian women was recorded by the Greek historian Herodotus. There are references to puppetry in the writings of Plato and Aristotle in ancient Greece. Human dolls with moveable limbs have been found in excavations dating from around 500 B.C.E. in Greece and in Greek colonies around the Mediterranean Sea, including Italy and North Africa.

Puppetry was well established in the era of the Roman Empire, but fell out of favor for a time in the early rise of Christianity when it was seen as a form of idolatry and a manifestation of the devil. Nonetheless, puppet performances as folk art for entertainment continued throughout the early Middle Ages in the hands of itinerant groups such as Gypsies. By the 14th century C.E., puppet shows with themes from the Bible, including enactments of the crucifixion of Christ, were encouraged by the Church and puppets were included in mystery and biblical plays performed by live actors. It has been suggested that the term "marionette," meaning "little Mary," may derive from the appearance of the Virgin Mary in medieval puppet performances.

Coincidentally, secular comic and satiric puppetry shows were also performed, sometimes by the same troupes that presented religious themes. In the succeeding centuries troupes using hand puppets, shadow puppets, and marionettes performing on small portable stages or wagons provided entertainment throughout Europe.

The history of puppetry in Russia spans many centuries. Hand puppets representing Petrouchka, the mischiefmaker, and a cast of entertaining characters date from the seventeenth century. Igor Stravinsky's ballet *Petrouchka* is based on these puppet shows. During and shortly after the Russian Revolution in the early 20th century, puppets were used for spreading propaganda in largely illiterate segments of Russian society. Professional puppet theaters were established in the 1920s in Russia, and many forms of puppetry flourished in the Soviet Union during and after World War II.

Puppetry also has a long history in the Near East and Asia. An ancient Sanskrit play includes a character identified as *Sutradhara*, "the holder of strings," who appears to be the oldest documented reference to puppets manipulated by strings. There is a strong tradition of puppetry in Central Asia and India, where articulated or non-articulated figures cut out of leather, wood, and other materials were used to cast shadows. This region is also home to an ancient tradition of puppets manipulated by strings and rods. The Chinese lantern shadow puppet theatre tradition, *pi-ying xi*, is at least 2000 years old.

Puppets have been used for rituals in North and South America for many centuries. Terracotta figures with articulated arms and legs were among artifacts found in excavated sites occupied by the Teotihuacan culture in Mexico, dated around 600 C.E. Ceremonies in which puppets played an important role have been documented in Central and South America, Alaska, the Pacific Northwest, Canada, and among Native American people in the United States.

CHAPTER ONE

Puppetry in Sub-Saharan Africa

Mythical Origins of Puppets

Many African cultures have different myths and stories that relate the origin of puppets in their communities. It is frequently reported that puppets appeared in dreams, during which they were delivered by deceased members of the community or spirits coming from the bush, the realm of the dead, the underworld or from beneath the water. In some versions of the myth or dream, a female figure brings a puppet or puppets to a man or directs a carver to create a puppet that is endowed with magical properties. Another story line involves the unexpected discovery of a mysterious object that is transformed into a puppet or leads to the creation of a puppet.

A myth from Malawi in West Africa incorporates a moral into the story of the origin of puppets. It recounts how an elderly man without offspring carved two small statues representing a boy and girl to fill the void of the children he missed. The man brought the statues home to show to his wife. At night, the statues mysteriously came to life, with the boy going out to hunt and the girl doing household chores. One day, the girl was severely chastised by the wife for failing to bring water from the river, and she began to cry loudly. Upon hearing his sister's distress, the boy also began to cry, and both children became inconsolable. Upon awaking the next morning, the man and his wife found that the children had been transformed back into statues.

A story from northern Togo traces the origin of puppets to fetishes or "small gods" that God created to help people communicate with Him. Over time, the priests responsible for addressing God through the fetishes were replaced by sacred wooden statues called *tchitchili*. These inarticulate, abstract statues with a human form are still used in the Moba region of northern Togo where they are employed as intermediaries to communicate with ancestors and as participants in initiation and farming rituals. *Tchitchili* are offered food, bathed, and may become encrusted with libations poured on them (1).

In Mali, one myth attributes the origin of *Sogo bò* puppets to a Boso fisherman who was taken by bush genies (*wòkulòw*) to their realm where he learned the occult art of making and performing puppets. Upon return to his village, the fisherman taught blacksmiths how to make puppets and create puppet shows. This story is consistent with the generally accepted understanding that the Malian puppet tradition originated with the Boso and Sòmonò people from whom it passed to Bamana and Maraka farming communities in the mid- to late-nineteenth century.

1. **Tchitchili,** the sacred anthropomorphic wooden figure of the Moba people in Togo, is used to communicate with ancestors as well as in farming and initiation rituals. H 32 in. Wood encrusted with libations.

The relationship between puppetry in ancient Egypt and North Africa and Sub-Saharan Africa is uncertain. A form of masquerade with features similar to a large, contemporary *Sogo bò* puppet, was described in 1352 by the Arab traveler, Ibn Battuta, at the court of Mansa Suleyman, the ruler of Mali. The event centered around the recitation of poems by poets who each appeared before the sultan inside the figure of a bird that resembled a thrush made of feathers with a wooden head and a red beak. Rod puppets with articulated bird heads were documented in Mali in the latter part of the 19th century, and they still constitute an important part of the *Sogo bò* tradition.

The oral history of the Ségou empire in the 18th century under its founder and leader, Biton Coulibaly, makes reference to the use of puppets in festivals. Biton Coulibaly is credited with having organized the youth associations that are now the keepers of the Malian puppet tradition.

From the writings of early European explorers, it is known that puppets existed in sub-Saharan Africa in the 17th century, and judging from the complexity of puppet performances reported by these observers, puppetry must have predated the European "discovery" of the continent by many years. There are published references to puppets during the European exploration of sub-Saharan Africa and after the advent of colonialism. In his book entitled *Journal of the Second Journey into Interior of Africa,* published in 1829, the explorer Hugh Clapperton described a multi-act performance in Nigeria that included the appearance of a large snake puppet constructed of cloth that was painted to resemble a boa constrictor. During the performance, the snake poked its head from a bag in which it was contained and opened its mouth in an attempt to bite an actor who protected himself by waving a sword at the snake's head. Appearing to be mortally wounded, the snake coiled itself and continued to strike out as it was carried away. Given the complexity of its movements and its size, this might have been a body puppet inhabited by one or more operators.

PUPPETS IN RITUALS

Puppets have long played an important role in protecting the community from social and occult dangers, as well as participating in divination, healing, sorcery, initiation, and funeral rituals throughout much of sub-Saharan Africa. The widespread use of puppets or puppet-like objects in these rites is further evidence of the existence of a centuries-old puppetry tradition in this region of the world. A few examples of these uses of puppets are described in this section.

Protecting Community Values

Gelede, a secret men's society of the Yoruba people in Benin and Nigeria, enacts ritual performances designed to protect the community by supporting social norms. The society performs plays and dances based on ancestral traditions. Important themes are the resolution of conflict through cooperation and the avoidance of violence. Daytime masquerades deal with issues of community and social concern such as jobs and professions, fashion, politics, and public health. Completely covered by a costume composed of brightly colored cloth strips, the performer wears a mask placed on top of his head like a cap, covering the upper part of his face. Situated on a bowl-shaped base, in the form of a strongly featured face, the upper part of the mask displays a carving that epitomizes the specific subject of the performance. Articulated puppets operated by the shrouded performer using strings are found on some *Gelede* masks, especially those of the Anago Yoruba people in Benin (2).

The central theme of other *Gelede* masquerades, especially those performed at night, is the celebration of women, whose creative power through giving birth and nurturing children is necessary for the prosperity of the community. In addition to wearing a traditional mask with facial features on top of his head, the performer's costume sometimes includes a protruding pair of breasts and a wooden body mask that represents a pregnant abdomen, upon which is situated a suckling infant in the form of an articulated puppet. The masquerade invokes the power of women and female ancestors to protect and bless the community and draws attention to the disastrous consequences for the society of failure to respect and honor women.

Divination

Divination is the practice of answering questions or foretelling the future that is usually revealed to a diviner with occult knowledge and supernatural power through the interpretation of omens and signs. Puppets are among various types of objects used by practitioners of divination in some sub-Saharan countries for communicating with the spirit world, often speaking with them in an unintelligible language or a strange voice.

A divination ritual, observed in Burkina Faso, employed a pair of small, copper, human male and female, non-articulated figures that were moved on the ground in a space about the size of a handkerchief like pawns in a game. The séance was conducted through a series of questions posed by the diviner who also delivered answers through ventriloquism. Having reached a conclusion, the diviner ended the session and offered his verdict.

The *Galukoshi* divination puppet-like object of the Pende people of the Democratic Republic of Congo consists of a small, painted, wood head with a feathered coiffure. The head is attached to an accordion-like wooden or bamboo handle that can be extended or retracted. The diviner detects the perpetrator of some transgression when the head shoots forward at the guilty person **(3)**.

Toe puppets are employed for divination and entertainment in a number of African nations. At the outset of the ritual, the diviner uses white clay to draw a rectangular, symbolic design on the ground. He places ritual objects within the marked space before seating himself on the ground with his feet in the sacred space and toes upright. The puppets are a pair of figures representing a man and a woman made of wooden sticks or strips of bamboo attached to a taut string looped around the operator's big toes. The diviner directs questions to the puppets and throws cowrie shells into the design drawn on the ground. By using the special knowledge imparted to him by ancestors as well as the spirits of powerful animals and sacred places, he is able to find answers to his questions by interpreting the movements of the puppets and the positions of the shells.

2. *Gelede* mask of the Anago Yoruba people in Benin. The articulated puppet figures on top of the head are moved by pulling the strings hanging below the mask. These strings would have been hidden by the performer's outfit. The puppets on this mask address the responsibility of a father (left) to raise his child (right). When the strings are pulled, the child is raised up and over the father's head, a literal expression of the subject of the mask. H 14 in. Wood, paint, string.

3. The ***Galukoshi*** divination puppet-like objects of the Pende people in the Democratic Republic of Congo consists of a small head with the facial features of a Pende mask. The head is attached to an accordion-like handle. H 9 in. Wood, bamboo, feathers, pigments, plant fibers.

Illness

Puppets have a long history of use in Sub-Saharan Africa for the diagnosis, treatment and cure of illness. They have served as a diagnostic aide, a role that has been described among the Mitsogho people of Gabon. Here, the medicine doctor consulted by a patient addressed questions about the illness to a small, sacred human statuette belonging to the secret *Bwiti* society. The patient was witness to the suspenseful, theatrical conversation between the doctor and the statuette. By interrogating his consultant puppet and listening closely to its answers, the doctor was able to offer a diagnosis, treatment, and prognosis for the patient.

In contemporary Mali, puppets have been used in the treatment of patients with psychiatric illness and for public health education programs directed at the control of AIDS. Public health campaigns against leprosy in Togo and malaria in the Central African Republic have employed puppets as a means of communication with the public.

Initiation

The *Kagba* puppet appears during the initiation of Senufo boys in Cote d'Ivoire. It consists of a rod puppet in the form of an antelope head protruding from a cloth-covered armature that represents the animal's body. A puppeteer within the armature moves the antelope's head and dances to set the entire construction in motion.

The Lega people in the Democratic Republic of Congo are known to use stringed puppets during initiation rites. Accompanied by a mocking song, the puppets are set in motion by recently circumcised boys to cast shame on those who were fearful of the procedure. The puppets consist of small wooden human figures with arms upraised, legs spread apart and slightly bent at the knees, and a grass skirt. Cowrie shells are embedded in the encrusted surfaces of the puppets.

Funerals

The *niombo* burial of a chief or important person of the Bwende people in the Democratic Republic of Congo involves a giant, puppet-like figure consisting of the mummified remains of a chief wrapped in many layers of cloth contributed by members of the deceased's clan. As described in 1957 by the Swedish missionary and ethnographer, K.E. Laman (quoted by Jacobson-Widding, 1979), after partly binding the body with cloth, the ritual attendants "...stretch out the arms, one pointing forward and the other upward. Red blanketing or a reddish cloth is now wound round the whole to give a living impression. A well-made head with cap is set on top, with eyes and a mouth and clearly visible teeth. Figures corresponding to the tattooing on the deceased are made on the face and on the body." The wrapped body, with limbs flexed in a dance pose, is carried in a procession accompanied by songs, the beating of gongs and drums, and gunfire through the village to the very large grave where the giant figure is interred in a standing or seated position. "Those carrying the corpse walk a few steps and then stop, as if the deceased was reluctant to go to the grave and wished to go home. One salvo after another is fired, and the procession resumes its march to the grave. Those in front may even turn around to go home again. But in this case the very youngest come to the edge of the road and turn, so to speak, the corpse in the direction of the grave again." (K.E. Laman, 1957; quoted by Jacobson-Widding, 1979).

Among the Bassar people of northern Togo, one finds a diminutive puppet (*unil*) made of woven, blackened plant fibers that substitutes for the body of a deceased woman during her second funeral rites. Wrapped in a funeral cloth and wearing a cowrie shell necklace, the puppet is placed on a bed of bamboo rods and covered with several traditional cloth skirts. The puppet is carried through the village at the head of a procession leading to its final resting place.

CHAPTER TWO

Our Introduction to Malian Puppets

In 2003, our fascination with Malian puppetry was sparked by a morning spent at the atelier of Yaya Coulibaly, a master puppet artist in Bamako, the capital of Mali. The experience of entering the workplace that is home to the artist, his family, their goats and dogs and to a myriad of puppets was truly extraordinary. We found ourselves surrounded by a vast array of human and animal puppet figures animated by colorful, expressively carved faces **(4)**. Many puppets were demonstrated for us including rod puppets, body puppets large enough to entirely enclose the performer and string puppets (marionettes) **(5-8)**. Coulibaly has likened entering a puppet body to returning to the womb to obtain maternal wisdom ("*nous pouvions entrer dans la marionette habitée comme si nous entrions dans le ventre de notre mère pour y sucer son savior*").

4

8

4. We found ourselves surrounded by a vast array of human and animal puppet figures animated by expressively carved faces in the atelier of Yaya Coulibaly. Bamako, Mali, 2003.

5. The body puppet of **Yayaroba**, a beautiful, morally correct woman in Yaya Coulibaly's atelier. Bamako, Mali, 2003.

6. One of Yaya Coulibaly's assistants begins to enter into the **Yayaroba** puppet by placing the supporting framework on his shoulders. One of two wooden rods used to move the puppet's arms is visible below the puppeteer's right elbow. Bamako, Mali, 2008.

7. **Yayaroba** towers above the completely covered performer and a visitor. Bamako, Mali, 2003.

8. Yaya Coulibaly brings a string puppet (marionette) to life at his atelier. Bamako, Mali, 2003.

In January 2008, we returned to Mali to attend puppet performances at the Festival sur le Niger in Ségou, a city on the bank of the Niger River. Before traveling to Ségou we spent several hours with Yaya Coulibaly and his performance troupe at his home and atelier in Bamako. It looked quite different from our visit in 2003. Walls had been removed and foundations were being laid to enlarge the structure with the goal of creating a museum and performance space. After a brief tour of the house, we were introduced to and shook hands with all of the members of the performance troupe **(9)** before we settled down to talk under a thatched roof in a courtyard filled with puppets and related apparatus in various states of repair and creation **(10)**. The space was animated by dogs, pet goats, the performers and puppet makers as well as construction workers. It was evident from the various carving tools, blocks of wood, and partially finished puppets in the space where we sat that this was at once a workshop as well as a gathering place for Coulibaly and his associates **(11, 12)**.

10

9

9. Yaya Coulibaly surrounded by his assistants and members of the Sogolon Puppet Troupe in the courtyard of his home. Bamako, Mali, 2008.

10. The courtyard of Yaya Coulibaly's home was filled with puppets and related apparatus. Bamako, Mali, 2008.

11. In this corner of Yaya Coulibaly's courtyard, we found a pile of shredded plastic used as a substitute for grass to make the skirt around the bottom of a *Sogo bò* puppet masquerade, an armature that supports this type of puppet masquerade, and aging blocks of wood used to carve puppets. Bamako, Mali, 2008.

12. Puppets are carved mainly with the tools shown here in Yaya Coulibaly's atelier: a small hammer and an adze. The sticks piled next to the partially visible antelope puppet are handles for puppets. Bamako, Mali, 2008.

The conversation quickly evolved into a lecture about Malian puppets that Coulibaly introduced with the comment that "…nothing is forbidden to them. They bring happiness and they are danced. They are the image of and offer criticism of daily life." He explained that puppets also serve as a bridge between the invisible, supernatural realm and the palpable world that people inhabit. Bringing a puppet to life, he observed, requires physical, mental and cultural training in order to support the weight, to understand the puppet's mind and to learn the secrets of how it moves. A member of the troupe demonstrated how he stooped to enter into a large puppet masquerade before he stood to bring it to an upright position **(13)**. Peter asked permission to look inside the puppet and examine how it was constructed but was told this was not permitted because he had not been initiated in the secrets that the puppet held.

In contrast to the large *Sogo bò* puppet masquerades we later saw performing in Ségou that were outfitted with straw skirts, most of those in Coulibaly's atelier had skirts made of recycled plastic strips, which he referred to as "plastic raffia" **(11, 13, 14)**. The utility of this contemporary adaptation to puppets transported for events in Mali and abroad became readily apparent in the Ségou performances, where it was necessary to sweep the space after each puppet was danced to remove loose straw.

13

14

13. One of Yaya Coulibaly's assistants has entered a *Sogo bò* antelope puppet masquerade and raised it by standing up. A male figure is seated between the antelope's horns. The masquerade has a voluminous skirt of shredded plastic. The puppeteer is able to see through the piece of white netting on the front. This puppet can be seen in repose in the right front of Figure **10**. Bamako, Mali, 2008.

14. Colorful strips of plastic are attached to the round armature that supports the skirt of a camel puppet demonstrated by one of Yaya Coulibaly's assistants. The armature is suspended from straps that pass over the puppeteer's shoulders. In performance the person would be covered by the remainder of the costume. Also shown is an antelope puppet head with brass appliqué and a male figure between its horns. This antelope is also seen in Figures **10** and **13**. Bamako, Mali, 2008.

Coulibaly explained that the straw skirt is a reference to puppets in the past that were constructed entirely of grass. He noted that the grass puppets are rarely found in collections or museums because they are very fragile and were usually burned after being danced to "foster procreation by the spirits" and enhance the harvest. This was an act of recycling in which the ashes symbolically reinvigorated the soil prior to planting. As outsiders, we would be allowed to observe grass puppets perform, but we would not be permitted to witness the sacred act of burning.

A theme Coulibaly stressed was the recycling of material for use in puppets, including plastic, cloth, rubber, wood, and metal. Imaginative use of discarded or found materials was evident in several puppets. One interesting example had an armature constructed from pipes. It was padded on the back with a traditional Malian man's shirt (*dloki* or *forokoni*) made from hand-woven cotton strips with a central band of blue and sides consisting of white hand-woven cotton cloth **(15, 16, 17)**.

Other informants told us that small puppets are sometimes outfitted with pieces of cloth given for this purpose by the wives of the puppet makers. Coulibaly observed that "…the men get the cloth from women and set it aside for making puppets."

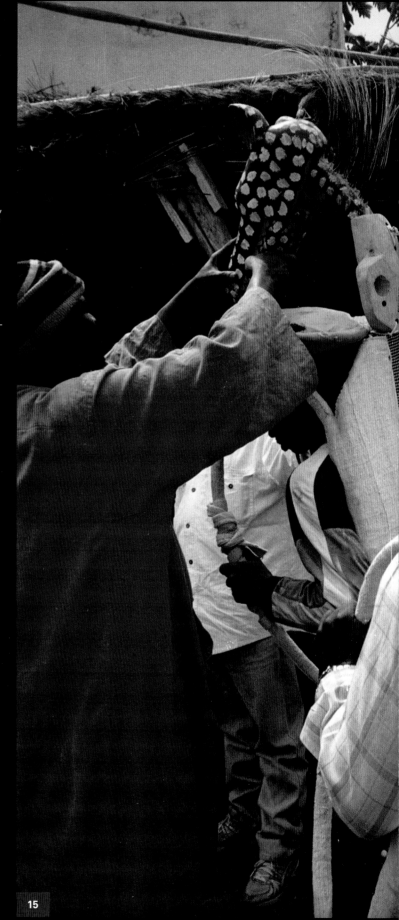

15. Yaya Coulibaly inserts a rod puppet head of **Nama**, the hyena, into an armature made from metal pipes. He is holding the mouth closed. A disc of yellow plastic is used to help support the cloth outfit that will envelope the puppeteer. The back of the armature is padded with a traditional men's cotton shirt or *dloki*. The shed with a grass roof and awning in the background is Yaya Coulibaly's workplace. Bamako, Mali, 2008.

16. This rod puppet is a rabbit. Bamako, Mali, 2008.

17. A *dloki* worn by Aldjouma Dolo on the bank of the Niger River. Ségou, Mali, 2008.

25

During the 2008 trip, we revisited the metal recycling market in Bamako. Here, many blacksmiths working with largely traditional methods fashion a fascinating array of utilitarian metal objects from the remnants of automobiles, trucks, bicycles, buses, refrigerators, 55-gallon drums, and other no-longer-recognizable sources (18). Most of the blacksmiths sit on low stools or logs hammering glowing red metal on anvils stuck in the ground or in a block of wood. An assistant cranks the wheel that powers a bellows to provide a draft of air to sustain the charcoal fire. Being in the midst of almost deafening clanging sounds produced by blacksmiths at work, the pungent pall of charcoal smoke and enormous physical energy dedicated to the creative recycling the iron, produced an unforgettable experience (19). Among the items for sale in the recycling market were hoes and plows similar to those used by puppets that are illustrated in this volume (20, 21).

18

19

18. Sheets of iron made from 55-gallon drums at the iron recycling market. Bamako, Mali, 2008.

19. A view of the iron recycling market. Bamako, Mali, 2008.

20. Hoes and household paraphernalia for sale at the iron recycling market. Bamako, Mali, 2008.

21. Plows for sale at the iron recycling market. Bamako, Mali, 2008.

Driving north from Bamako toward Ségou, we encountered herds of Zebu cattle along the road and scattered in the nearby bush. We stopped to admire their magnificent horns and the beautiful, random black and white patterns of their hides. In return, we were studied with equal intensity by many pairs of large, round eyes and were struck by how well the bush cow puppets in our collection captured the spirit of these animals **(22)**.

22

Most villages through which we passed had at least one Islamic mosque located near the paved road. Often, these structures were the tallest buildings to be seen. Some were finished with a smooth stucco surface and painted with one or more pastel colors that shone in the bright sun. Others were made of concrete or surfaced with mud. Although differing architecturally, each of the mosques had a finial affixed to the top of a dome or minaret. The most frequent finial form consisted of a five-pointed star and a crescent moon **(23-25)**. A less common type of finial consisted of a vertical rod or column surmounted by a crescent moon alone, a complete circle or a more complex assemblage of these forms **(26, 27)**. The crests on some of the bird puppets illustrated in this volume have forms that duplicate mosque finials, thus incorporating these important Islamic symbols into Bamana and Boso *Sogo bò* puppet masquerades.

As we neared Ségou, the road came closer to the Niger River. It was here that we encountered a shop with a roadside sign depicting the Nile perch, or *capitaine* fish, found in the Niger River. We also found a painting of the *capitaine* fish in a Niger River pirogue. The *capitaine* plays an important role in the diet and economy of the Boso people, and it is represented in *Sogo bò* theatre **(28-30)**.

23

24

27

25

26

22. Zebu cattle along the road from Bamako to Ségou, Mali, 2008.

23. A finial consisting of a star and crescent moon on the dome of a concrete mosque. Lightening rods are present below the dome. Mali, 2008.

24. A star and crescent moon finial adorns the dome of this mosque made of mud. The protruding wooden poles help to support the building, and they also serve as a scaffold to climb on when new mud is applied to the exterior. Mali, 2008.

25. A crescent moon finial on a painted mosque minaret built with cement blocks. Mali, 2008.

26. A circular finial on top of a domed mosque. Mali, 2008.

27. The conical dome on this concrete mosque is topped by a finial consisting of crescents, discs and stars. Mali, 2008.

VENTE DE POISSONS FRAIS
TOUTE SORTE
CHEZ BAYINI DJIRE
SEGOU
N°CELL/6156371
COURA

28. Peter Rosen outside a fish market where the sign depicts a Nile perch or *capitaine* fish that is indigenous to the Niger River. Ségou, Mali, 2008.

29. The image of a *capitaine* fish painted inside a pirogue on the Niger River. Mali, 2003.

30. Capitaine fish for sale in Ségou, Mali, 2008.

CHAPTER THREE

The Sogo Bò Puppet Theatre Tradition

The Bamana and Boso People

Ségou, a small city in south central Mali, is the center of the rich and evolving tradition of masked and puppet theatre performed in many surrounding rural villages, where life depends mainly on farming, raising cattle, and fishing. The performances are referred to as *nyènajè*, meaning a spectacle or celebration, a term that underscores their festive or secular nature despite their origin in animistic religious traditions. The theatre honors, appeases, and appeals to traditional spirits to protect the community by ensuring abundant rain, crops, and fish.

The festivals coincide with the beginning and end of the farming and fishing cycles, preceding the onset of the rainy season in the Spring and the end of the harvest in the Fall. The organizers of these events are the Bamana (Bambara) and Maraka people, who are farmers and traders, and Boso and Sòmonò people, who depend on fishing for their livelihood. For simplicity, these groups will be referred to here as Bamana and Boso. The timing of festivals may differ slightly from one village to another or between Bamana and Boso communities, but today Bamana and Boso festivals often occur jointly.

The Bamana and Boso people are part of the large Mande cultural group that is present across much of West Africa. Bamana and Boso villages and towns are widely distributed in western, eastern, and south central Mali. Bamana communities in the region, roughly extending from Bamako, the capital of Mali, to Djènnè in the north, have had the greatest contact with Boso fishing communities located on the banks and islands in the Niger River in this region, as well as to the west along the Senegal River in the Kayes region of Mali. The Bamana refer to the Boso as the *Jitigi*, masters of the water. These groups live in closely related communities and have had considerable influence on each other, resulting in many common cultural customs including the mask, puppet, and masquerade theatre described in this book.

Islam became established as the core religion over several centuries throughout Mali and most of the surrounding countries of sub-Saharan Africa. In this region, Islam coexists with traditional animistic religious beliefs of the Bamana and Boso people that revolve around spirits or genies representing the forces of nature. The cosmology of the Bamana and Boso people encompasses the observable world of everyday experience and an unseen realm inhabited by spirits. In this context, a harmonious society is one that provides a means for carefully adjusting social norms over time, while at the same time maintaining contact with the traditional spirit world through objects such as masks and puppets.

Religious societies within Bamana and Boso communities, probably predating the introduction of Islam, have not only been protectors of the community by serving as intermediaries between people and the spirits, but they also have had a strong influence on the social and political life of the community. Traditional ceremonies performed by these societies for initiation, to maintain social order, and for other purposes have for centuries employed masks, statues, and altars endowed with sacred powers.

Animistic spirits of most concern to the Bamana have been those involved with activities such as farming and hunting on the lands they occupy. On the other hand, the ancestral spirits of the Boso people are connected to water and fish. Central themes of the religious rites of both groups are to protect and sustain the community by interceding with spirits to provide an abundant harvest of grain or fish as well as seeking protection for farmers, hunters, and fishermen. As recounted in their myths, the current mask and puppetry theatre of the Bamana and Boso people are a continuation of long-standing animistic religious practices that have evolved and acquired a significant secular component during at least a century in Mali.

Responsibility for performing and perpetuating the *Sogo bò* theatre tradition is vested in an association or *ton* in Bamana and Boso communities. Members of the association are referred to as *ton den*, the children of the association. The leader of the association is the *tontigi*. The association has a meeting house referred to as the *tonso*. The *ton* traditionally includes all village boys and young men ranging in age from approximately fourteen to their mid-thirties, but more recently it has also involved girls from fourteen years until they are married. The *ton* is organized by age groups whose members develop life-long bonds akin to those formed in a fraternity. Through their participation in the *ton*, members of the association learn the rules, values and traditions of community life as well as respect for their elders and the importance of socially beneficial, cooperative effort. In rural communities, an integral part of this educational process is learning the importance of teamwork through group activities such as farming to produce crops that are sold to fund mask and puppet theatre performances. Members of the *ton* may also help elderly or infirm individuals who need assistance in the community, and they may participate in community-based public works. Masks and puppets belong to the youth association and are kept in a communal sanctuary.

Women are excluded from the wearing of masks and the performance of puppets, but they are responsible for the accompanying songs and they play musical instruments except for drums. Young male members of the *ton* are taught the secrets of the mask and puppet theatre by their elders. They learn the names of animals and spirits, their myths and mystical powers, as well as the songs and music with which they are identified. Through this process, the youth become familiar with their cultural and religious heritage and learn to assume the responsibilities that come with adulthood.

Traditionally, masks and puppets were commissioned from a blacksmith by the *ton*. According to Bamana mythology, the blacksmith— or *numu*—was the first human to have been created. *Numu* belong to a separate caste because of the occult knowledge that they employed in the past to extract iron from the soil and their ability to create from raw metal their valued objects, such as tools, weapons, and jewelry. A subset of blacksmiths, the *kulew* or cutters of wood, carve masks, puppets and utilitarian objects such as mortars, pounders, door locks, and stools. Today, carvers may also be blacksmiths in the village setting, but carvers who are not blacksmiths can be found in Malian villages and cities.

The form of a mask or sculpture may be based on a design provided by the *ton*; it might be copied from an existing form or it could be a creation inspired by the blacksmith's imagination to fulfill a commission to devise a puppet for a new topic. The act of creating these sculptures has special significance because they are objects endowed with spiritual energy and power given to them by the carver.

In its raw form, the sculpture, made from a relatively easy to carve lightweight wood, is white. Old puppets were darkened or colored with natural dyes and decorated with materials such as mirrors, metal appliqué, and cloth. For many decades, bright paints have been used to "sweeten" and enhance the visibility of new sculptures. Surviving old unpainted masks and puppets are also sometimes painted if their original decoration has deteriorated or simply to bring them up-to-date.

Masks, puppets, and puppet masquerades employed in the *Sogo bò* theatre are performance objects that are used by performers who are hidden from the audience. Technically, a mask differs from a puppet in that it is attached to and moves in the same plane or space as the person who wears it, whereas a puppet occupies a space separate from the person who sets it in motion; as a result it has greater freedom of movement. This strict distinction is confounded in some instances by masks with articulated parts that may be set in motion by the movements of the dancer. In the *Sogo bò* theatre, masks and puppets are regarded as two sides of a coin, since they both serve as a means for communicating between the invisible realm of the supernatural and the world of humankind. In this context, no formal distinction is made between masks and puppets in the *Sogo bò* theatre.

In this presentation, we refer to three types of performance objects. 1) Figures wearing masks are identified as **masked performers** or **masks**. We have chosen to distinguish between 2) **puppets** as performance objects in the form of single rod figures, articulated figures or busts, and 3) **puppet masquerades** as complex performance objects in which a mask or puppet is supported by or attached to an armature covered with cloth, straw or shredded plastic surrounding one or more hidden performers.

Sogo (*sogow*, plural) is the Bamana word for antelope that is generalized in this context to represent all types of animals as well as spirits or genies of the bush, human characters, and certain concepts that are represented by masks, puppets, and masquerades. *Sogo* is also a term for a large animal masquerade figure that serves as a mobile stage, the *Sogoba*, surrounding puppeteers who manipulate small puppets. The entire performance or event is referred to as *Sogo bò*, "the animals come forth" in some Bamana communities; whereas others refer to the masquerades as *Cèko*, meaning the affairs of men. Among the Boso and Sòmonò people, terms such as *Do bò*, "the secrets come forth," or *Jikando*, "the mystery of the water," are sometimes used. In order to simplify this presentation, we have chosen to refer to the entire repertoire of masks, puppets, and puppet masquerades as *Sogo bò* theatre.

Performances are animated by lively music and songs sung by a chorus of women with a lead female singer. The song chosen for a particular mask, puppet or puppet masquerade is one appropriate to the character being presented. The identity of the character, the story being enacted, and the metaphor it embodies are conveyed in the lyrics, movements of the performer, and music. Drums played by men are the dominant musical instruments. The beat created by the drummers is augmented by other instruments, such as the African flute, the rhythmic clapping of hands, the shaking of calabash rattles containing seeds or adorned by glass beads or cowrie shells in loose netting, and the clacking sound of wooden, hand-held clappers (*tègèrèw*) manipulated by the female chorus. The singers and musicians select a rhythm, or *dùn*, suitable to the character being performed. A slow rhythm accompanies the appearance of *Faro*, a female water genie, and *Yayaroba*, the beautiful woman who moves gracefully to a languorous, slow-paced song. Puppets that represent large animals such as *Sama* the elephant, *Ntilen* the giraffe, and *Waraba* the lion are usually accompanied by faster rhythms.

Sogo bò theatre provides a vehicle for young men and women to offer social criticism that may not otherwise be easily expressed on the relationships between individuals and the community, youth and their elders, men and women, and of people within the spirit world. This situation is succinctly summarized in the following comments by Marie Kruger, Chair of the Drama Department at Stellenbosch University in South Africa:

> Traditional practices in Africa are amongst the many potential problems addressed by theatre as a tool for social change.... To question behavior patterns that have been handed down over generations is no easy task.... Authoritative recipients of tradition may have elevated certain rules, beliefs, and norms of the past to a level of authority not because of their usefulness for the present, but because of their pastness as such.... (Kruger in NTQ, p. 331).

Performances employ a cast of characters, songs and music that are familiar to the audience. However, the theatre has of necessity evolved and in some cases broken with tradition as new figures and topics have been added; others are no longer performed as social conditions have changed. The process of ongoing adjustment is manifested in the timing of festivals, the financing of the events as well as in the songs and performance objects. In some circumstance, the migration of young people to cities has necessitated the reinvention of the *ton* in an urban setting where the cost of putting on the festival cannot be covered by the sale of grain grown in communal fields. Because more people are employed at jobs during the week, the festival might be scheduled over a weekend, whereas traditionally other considerations may have been paramount. Over time, the existing masks, puppets, and masquerades are repainted, refreshed with new cloth, or modified to adjust the presentation to contemporary subjects and issues, and new forms are added to the repertoire for this purpose as well. As a consequence, *Sogo bò* puppet theatre serves as a mirror that reflects the evolution of the community. Specific masks, puppets or masquerades may be performed in one village or region but not in another. In some instances, the names associated with characters also differ among villages and regions. In so far as we can determine, the identification of mask and puppet characters included in this volume corresponds to nomenclature used in Ségou and the surrounding region from which we believe the majority of the masks and puppets originate.

THE SETTING

Bamana *Sogo bò* theatre festivals are centered on an open area or plaza in the village where the appearance of masks, puppets and puppet masquerades is usually preceded by various dances involving young men and women from the community and youth association. This part of the festival begins with a circle dance, in which men and women form concentric circles. A men's acrobatic competition to rapidly accelerating drumming often follows the circle dance. Clowns, the **Koredugaw**, dressed in strange outfits decorated with odd attachments, cavort in the arena during the preliminary events and sometimes during interludes between puppet performances **(31, 32)**. In addition to similar land-based dance activities, portions of Boso festivals occur in the river and near the shore, where water-borne puppets and masquerades appear in traditional boats, the pirogues.

Preparation of the masks, puppets and puppet masquerades for performance occurs in a shielded area near the site of the festival. This is a ritual process that is intended to keep the secrets of how the puppets are manipulated from the uninitiated and to hide the identities of the performers.

The first puppets, masks or puppet masquerades appear during the day and the festival continues after sunset. More than twenty masks, puppets, and puppet masquerades are presented sequentially in scenes, each lasting from five to fifteen minutes. The performances are accompanied by music, especially drumming, and songs sung by a female chorus. Musical interludes punctuate intervals between masquerades.

38

Masks, Puppets and Puppet Masquerades

Characters represented by masks, puppets, and puppet masquerades appear either separately or in combinations. However, masked figures rarely appear in the same scenes as puppets and puppet masquerades. Some animals are accompanied by an actor who is not disguised by a mask. One example is *Gòn*, the irreverent monkey who is represented by a masked performer dressed in torn sackcloth and is restrained on a leash held by an unmasked attendant.

Sogo bò puppet masquerades are accompanied by one or more attendants who assist the performers. Dancers covered by a masquerade are directed by an attendant who rings a small bell or taps the masquerade with a switch. Depending on the size and complexity of the masquerade, one or more other attendants positioned at the side or rear may also speak quietly to give guidance to the dancers as well as adjust the textiles covering it. They also pick up debris that has fallen from the puppet's skirt and help to keep the audience out of the way. The act of clearing the dance area between scenes also marks a change in rhythm and serves to sweep away evil spirits.

31. This ***Kòrèduga*** clown is standing with a horse puppet between his legs. The head of the horse is decorated with appliquéd brass. Strings of beads hang from the man's hunter's cap with horns. He is wearing a long necklace and a *dloki* made from hand woven, indigo colored cloth. A small, traditional hoe hangs from his right shoulder. A woman on the left is wearing printed cotton cloth with a black and white *bogolon* design. Ségou, Mali, 2008.

32. Another ***Kòrèduga*** clown in motion with many objects attached to his outfit including long strings of beads. His cap is decorated with cowrie shells and feathers. He is carrying a calabash rattle. Another performer is wearing a Santa Claus hat. The chorus of women in the background is singing, clapping hands, and shaking calabash rattles. Ségou, Mali, 2008.

A puppet masquerade is built around an armature made from flexible wooden, plastic or metal rods that are lashed together **(33, 34)**. The structures are large enough to completely cover one or more puppeteers who are hidden by cloth placed over the top of the armature and a fringe or skirt made from grass or shredded plastic strips. The top as well as the ends and sides of the body are draped with decorative cloth sheets, traditional blankets, and sometimes an Islamic prayer rug. The completed puppet masquerade, or *sogoba,* is a mobile stage that represents the body of an animal associated with land outside the village, the bush, or an animal that inhabits the water.

Wooden face, helmet and crest masks representing human, animal or spirit characters are typically specific to *Sogo bò*, but face masks such as *Ntomo* associated with men's initiation may also appear as reminders of these long-standing traditions. *Ntomo* is an association composed of boys prior to circumcision and initiation into adult associations, such as the *Koré* society. During a period of training to assume adult responsibilities, the boys learn the importance of controlling one's speech in order to keep secrets in preparation for acquiring sacred knowledge in later stages of initiation. The *Ntomo* mask consists of a face topped by a comb-like structure and sometimes by a female figure **(35)**. Cowrie shells, seeds, and brass or aluminum metal appliqué attached to the surface are used to enhance the power of the mask.

33

34

35

33. This *Sogo bò* puppet masquerade armature in Yaya Coulibaly's courtyard was made of bent wooden rods lashed together with cords. Plastic raffia is piled behind the armature. Bamako, Mali, 2008.

34. Two basket-shaped *Sogo bò* puppet masquerade armatures in Yaya Coulibaly's courtyard. Bamako, Mali, 2008.

35. A contemporary **Ntomo** mask in performance. The painted, white motif on the mask's comb-like superstructure probably represents cowrie shells that are affixed to the spines of a traditional **Ntomo** mask. Ségou, Mali, 2008.

Large rod puppets are usually part of the complex *sogoba* masquerade assemblage. They consist of an animal head attached to the armature by a wooden rod and manipulated by a dancer hidden inside the cloth body of the character. In addition to the supporting rod, strings may be attached to animate articulated parts of the animal head, such as the ears and mouth or secondary puppets situated on the animal's head or horns. These large animal heads emerge from the front end of the puppet masquerade's body. Rods and strings are used to hold and manipulate small rod puppets, the *sogoden* (children of the animal) *or maani* (little people), that emerge from the back of the *sogoba*. Small rod puppets representing human or animal characters may also be situated on the head and horns of the animal head at the front of the *sogoba*.

Large body puppets usually represent human characters. They consist of a head attached to a rod and a cloth body that entirely covers the performer. The arms and hands that emerge from the cloth body are manipulated by using rods held by the performer **(6)**.

A rod puppet is a performance object consisting of the head of an animal or person carved from a single piece of wood. The animal heads often have articulated parts, such as ears or a mouth, that are moved by strings. Some rod puppets of human characters include a bust. Rod puppets of human characters consisting only of a head are typically held in a performer's hand, whereas those with a bust usually have a base and are supported by the head or shoulders of the performer.

A particular type of female rod puppet with small, secondary puppets attached to its head, shoulders or both is referred to as the "mère des marionettes," or mother of the puppets with her children. The mother of puppets is displayed and carried by adults but is not danced during a performance. It represents the responsibility of the elders to oversee the cultural education of the young members of the community.

Puppets of the marionette type that are suspended by strings and operated from above are found in sub-Saharan Africa, including Mali **(8, 36-39)**, but they are rarely used in traditional *Sogo bò* puppet theatre.

Masked performers disguised by cloth outfits appear as a variety of characters in *Sogo bò* theatre. Masked figures are an integral part of the *Sogo bò* festival. The masked performances are so intimately enmeshed with the sequence of puppets that they are readily accepted as another form of puppetry in which the mask and costume serve as a body puppet that is inhabited by the dancer.

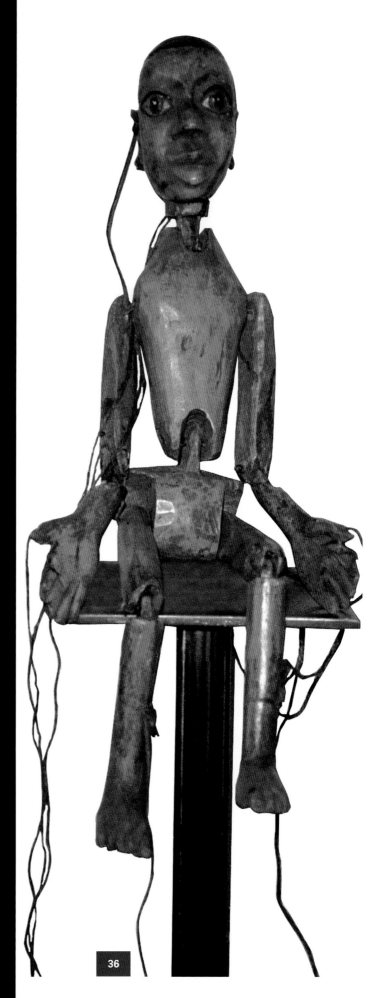

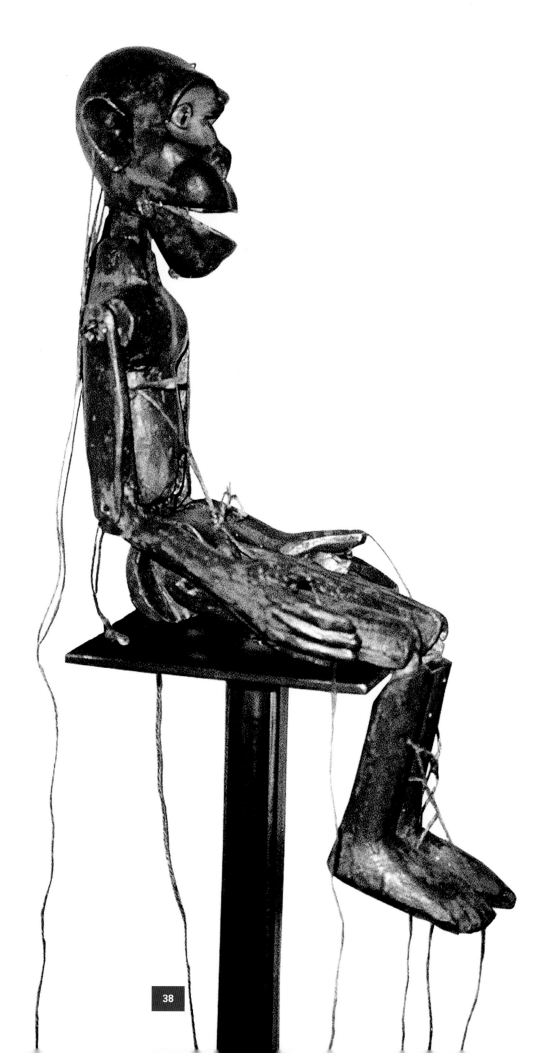

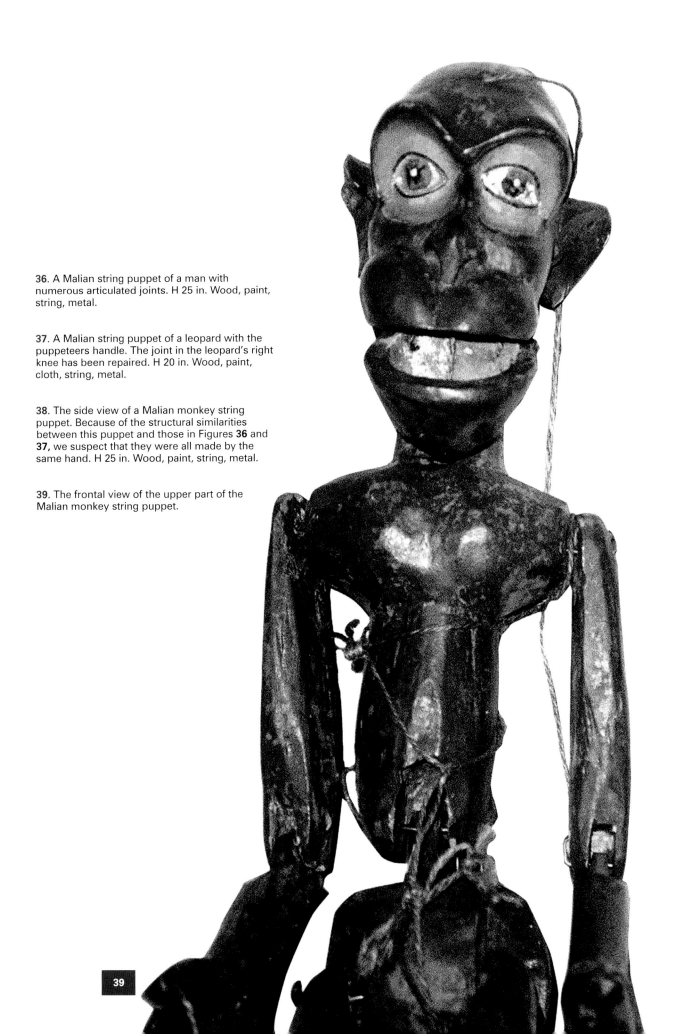

36. A Malian string puppet of a man with numerous articulated joints. H 25 in. Wood, paint, string, metal.

37. A Malian string puppet of a leopard with the puppeteers handle. The joint in the leopard's right knee has been repaired. H 20 in. Wood, paint, cloth, string, metal.

38. The side view of a Malian monkey string puppet. Because of the structural similarities between this puppet and those in Figures **36** and **37,** we suspect that they were all made by the same hand. H 25 in. Wood, paint, string, metal.

39. The frontal view of the upper part of the Malian monkey string puppet.

40

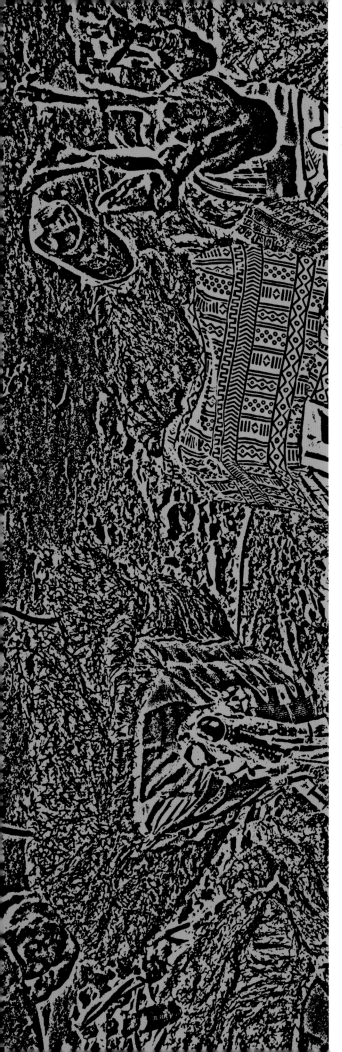

CHAPTER FOUR

Bamana Sogo Bò Theatre, 2008

The performances that we attended in 2008 were part of the fourth "Festival sur le Niger," a three-day event in the city of Ségou. The dance space for Bamana masks and puppets, the "Chapiteau," was a square of hard-packed clay shielded by a large tent with a central aperture through which a shaft of bright sunlight illuminated the performers. The puppets were energized by amplified music played by men and songs dramatically sung by a lead woman supported by a chorus of women who punctuated the music with rhythmic clapping of their hands, rattles, and the staccato sound of clappers. Some dancers who wore masks and cloth outfits performed to the music without assistants. The large *Sogo bò* puppet masquerades made of cloth and grass were accompanied by male attendants, including a leader who directed the puppet with signals from a small bell or stick. One or more other assistants kept the enthusiastic crowd of spectators from encroaching on the performance space, cleared the area of straw detached from the skirt, and adjusted textiles draping the puppet when they came loose.

The movements of each *Sogo bò* puppet masquerade consisted of a stylized dance choreographed to evoke the characteristic motion and spirit of the particular animal. The bodies of the animals were large enough to cover the one or more men who were hidden from view by a thick skirt of straw and textiles draped over the figure's back.

One of the most enchanting masked performances was that of a Fulani man and woman **(40-43)**. The female figure, taller than life-size, wore a mask painted golden yellow that was surmounted by a bowl decorated with green, yellow and red bands representing the Malian national colors. Her face displayed a happy countenance with a broadly smiling mouth. She was covered from her neck to her feet in a dark, loose cotton print dress, and her ample bosom bobbed under her clothing as she gracefully danced for the audience. It seemed likely that there was a mechanism beneath her garments that assisted her in achieving this effect. The shorter, male figure wore a mask with a pink painted face highlighted by a white goatee and topped by a carved, traditional Malian hat. The painted expression on the man's mask seemed to mirror his movements to display a range of emotions from surprise and amusement to concern and uncertainty. A short stick carried by the man was used very effectively for emphasis. In this dance, the woman was flirtatious, coy, proud, and appeared to enjoy being courted, but she showed her displeasure when the man attempted to pat her bottom. At the conclusion of the dance, the woman knelt so that the man could lean over and drink from the bowl on her head, a gesture symbolic of the life-sustaining role of women and possibly a metaphor for allegiance to Mali as the motherland. This amusing performance elicited an enthusiastic response from the audience, especially children who seemed to enjoy the mimicry of adult behavior.

41

42

43

40. A Fulani couple as masked performers. Ségou, Mali, 2008.

41. The Fulani man's outfit included a traditional Malian hat. Ségou, Mali, 2008.

42. The bowl on the woman's head has green, yellow, and red rings, the Malian national colors. The dark line around her mouth probably represents indigo tattooing. Ségou, Mali, 2008.

43. Near the end of the performance, the woman knelt to allow the man to drink from the bowl on her head. This sequence may represent the role of women who are the providers of food for the family as well as a metaphor for Mali as the motherland. Ségou, Mali, 2008.

Yayaroba, a beautiful woman of high moral standards who represents the epitome of womanhood, appeared several times representing different communities. The *Yayaroba* from Pélengana, a suburb of Ségou, and her jealous husband, *Jinèkaafiri,* appeared as masked figures **(44, 45)**. This *Yayaroba*'s large bosom was evident beneath a voluminous gown of blue printed cloth that matched the color of her mask. The combined height of the mask and the elaborate coiffure designed like a crown caused her to be noticeably taller than her husband. Perhaps to make up for his lesser stature, *Jinékaafiri* carried a stick with which he attempted (without success) to control his wife's movements. His unattractive appearance highlighted by an open mouth full of oversized teeth, a red face topped by three pairs of horns, and a bulging abdomen beneath a red robe was the antithesis of *Yayaroba*'s elegant, composed beauty.

The *Yayaroba* from another town displayed her bosom as a separate attachment through a gap in her printed cloth robe. She towered above the surrounding attendants because the mask she wore was elevated above the performer's head **(46)**.

44. **Yayaroba** from Pélengana, a suburb of Ségou, and her jealous, bearded husband, **Jinèkaafiri**, as masked performers. Ségou, Mali, 2008.

45. **Jinèkaafiri** with his stick. Note straw on the ground that came off the skirt of a previous *Sogo bò* puppet masquerade. The man leaning against the tent pole is an attendant to the performers. **Yayaroba**, the chorus, and the musicians are in the background. Ségou, Mali, 2008.

46. A tall *Yayaroba* towers above her attendants in the staging area before she enters the performance space. The mat made of woven grass in the background was used to shield puppets and masquerades from the audience. Ségou, Mali, 2008.

47. A horseman charges toward the audience. Ségou, Mali, 2008.

48. Two horsemen, *Les Soyaban de Pélengana*. One of the figures is resting on the left. Ségou, Mali, 2008.

Two horsemen, ***Les Soyaban de Pélengana***, wearing traditional Malian hats, who entered the arena astride horse puppets to the loud beating of drums, caused a big commotion as straw flew in all directions. Each horseman's face was covered by a cloth mask notable for a prominent, pointed nose and black, beady eyes **(47, 48)**. The horse puppets were mounted between the riders' legs in the fashion of ***Koredugaw***, horse puppets that are described in detail elsewhere in this book (see page **36**). The brightly painted horse-heads featured large flared nostrils and prominent eyes. Sheets of brightly colored cotton print cloth were draped on the horsemen and on the backs of the horses over voluminous skirts of straw that hid the performers' legs from view. After energetically dancing together, the horsemen took turns alternately resting on their haunches and dancing. From time to time, one of the horsemen would suddenly advance toward the audience, creating a stir as spectators, many of them children, shouted and retreated.

Animals in the form of *Sogo bò* puppet masquerades included ***Bakòrò***, the ram **(49)**; ***Nama***, the hyena **(50)**; ***So***, the horse **(51, 52)**; ***Waraba,*** the lion **(53)**; ***Mali Kònò***, the great bird of Mali **(54)**; several antelope **(55, 56)***;* and ***Sama***, the elephant **(57-59)**. The elaborately painted head of the elephant was surmounted by a bird, giving reference to the relationship between elephants and birds in the wild. Much of the elephant's upper body was covered by a white sheet and a large, cotton, Djerma-style blanket with a multicolored, checkerboard design typically found in Mali and neighboring countries. A thick layer of straw formed the skirt. The movements of the ***Sama*** puppet masquerade were directed by an attendant whose signals were spoken or transmitted by a small bell.

Placed in the middle of ***Sama's*** back was a small, male puppet *(maani)* wearing a conical red cap and dressed in print cloth. The small puppet's face and neck were painted yellow and his hands were painted red. When the elephant masquerade entered the arena, the recumbent ***maani*** was not visible. After a few minutes, the ***maani*** abruptly stood up and began gesturing with his articulated arms, as his body swayed with the elephant's movement. The sudden appearance of the small ***maani*** puppet on the back of the elephant was greeted by children with enthusiastic shouts of delight.

49 In this puppet masquerade **Bakòrò**, the ram, has a beard of colorful cotton strings and brass appliqué on his elaborately painted face. Ségou, Mali, 2008.

50. The neck and head of **Nama**, the hyena, are made of painted cloth and the armature that forms the body is entirely covered with grass. An elegant, flexible tail is attached at the rear. In *Sogo bò* puppet theatre the hyena is a metaphor for the complexity of human conduct. In some situations, it is praised as a powerful and smart hunter, whereas other performances draw attention to its shameless misbehavior. Ségou, Mali, 2008.

51. The *Sogo bò* puppet masquerade of **So**, the horse, from the town of Wéléntigila, leaves the staging area assisted by the man in the foreground. The cloth-covered rod extending to the right border of the image is one arm of the *maani* puppet of a man that is lying flat on the back of the horse. Ségou, Mali, 2008.

52. The *maani* puppet has risen and rides standing on the back of the horse. Ségou, Mali, 2008.

53. *Waraba*, the lion, with a flowing mane and long beard appears as a *Sogo bò* puppet masquerade. Ségou, Mali, 2008.

54. *Mali Kònò*, the great bird of Mali, with a fenestrated casque on the upper surface of its articulated beak, is the mythical national bird based on the hornbill bird. A replica of a mosque finial rises from the head of the bird. A printed *bogolan* cloth is draped over the bird's body. The man on the left is the attendant who directed *Mali Kònò*. Ségou, Mali, 2008.

55

56

57

58

59

55. The animals situated on the horns of **Dajè**, the roan antelope, a *Sogo bò* puppet masquerade from Pélengana, are crocodiles. Small puppets of two women seated on the back of the antelope are pounding grain. One woman is carrying a baby on her back. Note the similarity between the cloth used to drape the antelope and the outfit worn by the attendant on the left. Ségou, Mali, 2008.

56. Here **Dajè**, the roan antelope, has two sets of horns. The more posterior pair is carved in the form of *ciwara*, the mythical roan antelope that taught the Bamana people how to farm. The antelope's long, white beard is a symbol of wisdom. A white bird puppet is standing on **Dajè's** back. Ségou, Mali, 2008.

57. This *Sogo bò* puppet masquerade depicts **Sama**, the elephant, with a bird on the crown of its head. This side of the body is draped in a traditional cotton blanket with a multicolored, checkerboard design over a white cotton sheet and a grass skirt. A small male puppet with articulated arms stands on the elephant's back. The hand of the lead attendant holding a bell is visible on the left. Ségou, Mali, 2008.

58. The bird perched on **Sama**'s head may be a reference to the cooperative relationship between the elephant and birds such as the red billed oxpecker (*Buphagus erythrorhynchus*) that picks ticks, mites, and other insects off the elephant's back. Ségou, Mali, 2008.

59. The puppet (**Maani**) standing on the elephant has outstretched arms. Part of a decorative *bogolan* textile is present on this side of the puppet masquerade's body. Ségou, Mali, 2008.

One of the most spectacular puppet masquerades was an antelope from the town of Pélengana identified as *Madanitile*, the sun of Madani **(60)**. It was carved by Modibo Kulubali and named after his father, Madani, a famous carver. Sprouting at different angles from the crown of the head were multiple horns. Each of the central, vertical pair of horns terminated in a similarly painted small replica of the main antelope head except that a star found on the forehead of the latter was replaced by a small white disc representing the sun. Rising from the center of the antelope's forehead between the vertical horns was a slender post to which were attached symbols typically found on the finials of mosques, in the forms of a crescent moon, a star and a discoid sun, all painted white. Hanging from lateral horns were small fish painted white with black spots. Affixed to the backs of the most posterior horns were a pair of red crocodiles also with black spots. The antelope's mouth supported an ample white beard, a symbol of wisdom.

Ncona de Pélengana, a masquerade that combined human and animal features, had a white mask highlighted by a large, black moustache, bushy black eyebrows, the erect ears of an animal, an abundant white mane, and a long, mobile tail **(61)**. His body consisted of grass that was partly covered by sheets of colorful cloth. *Ncona* is a mythical man able to transform himself into a wild animal that terrorizes villages and kills people. This masquerade is a metaphor for a morally unstable person who is not faithful in marriage. Mythical bush spirits were also represented by masked figures in performances at night **(62, 63)**.

Adjacent to the tent was a staging area where the Bamana puppets and puppet masquerades were kept between performances. A fence of woven straw had been erected to hide the puppets from view. The doorway to this space, guarded by attendants, was opened only long enough to permit masked characters and puppet masquerades to exit and return. After some discussion, we persuaded the manager of a puppet troupe to let us into the staging area for a close-up look at the puppets in "repose." Most of the puppets were covered with cloth to keep them hidden when not being performed. One at a time, the cloths were briefly drawn back so that we could view each puppet. Because he was not initiated into the "secrets" of the puppets, Peter's request to see the inside of a puppet and to "try one on" was denied. At the conclusion of the day's festivities, the covered puppets were transported away from the staging area in a pick-up truck accompanied by performers and attendants **(64)**.

61

60. This antelope puppet masquerade named *Madanitile*, meaning "The Sun of Madani", was created by Modibo Kulubali in honor of his father Madani, a famous carver. The head has multiple horns with secondary animals as well as representations of the Islamic symbols for the moon and stars. Ségou, Mali, 2008.

61. *Ncona de Pélengana,* who appears as a puppet masquerade, is a mythical man with a large, black beard and bushy eyebrows. *Ncona* terrorizes the village because he can transform himself into a wild animal and kill people. His most prominent animal features are upright ears, a white mane, and a long tail. He is a metaphor for a morally unstable person who has a very disruptive effect on society or an unfaithful spouse whose behavior is damaging to a family. Ségou, Mali, 2008.

62. Bush spirits appear in a nocturnal dance as masks with avian features that are decorated with cowrie shells and white feathers. A musician is playing a balaphone just behind the dancers. Calabashes that serve as resonators beneath the balaphone protrude between small Malian flags hanging in front of the instrument. Ségou, Mali, 2008.

63. The bush spirit mask on the left has a bird-like beak. Feathers appear as the decorative motif on the *bogolan* cloth costumes. Ségou, Mali, 2008.

64. Cloth-covered *Sogo bò* puppet masquerades accompanied by attendants leave the performance area. The tall fence of woven grass in the background was used to shield the staging area where the puppets were hidden from the audience. Ségou, Mali, 2008.

65

CHAPTER FIVE

Boso Sogo Bò Theatre, 2008

Most of the Boso puppets and puppet masquerades from the town of Kirango were performed in 2008 on a sandy beach at the edge of the Niger River. Others were carried by pirogues in the river. All were accompanied by a lead woman singer, a chorus of women who sang and clapped, and men who played drums, stringed instruments, a balaphone and bells. Cloth sheets shielded the Boso puppets from view as they approached the performance area and immediately following the dance. On land, Boso *Sogo bò* puppet masquerades were guided by attendants including a leader who used a small bell for signaling and others who kept the perimeter clear.

Bala, the porcupine **(65)**, was made entirely from grass, whereas other puppet masquerades consisted of cloth stretched over an armature. The masquerades, maneuvered by a prone performer contained within the cloth body, included *Bama*, the crocodile **(66)**, *Goson*, the scorpion, and *Sa*, the snake **(67, 68)**. The snake drew loud cheers from the audience when it accomplished the remarkable feat of simultaneously raising its head and tail vertically in the air. In shallow water near the shore, two pirogues each carried a large rectangular *Sogo bò* puppet masquerade draped with printed textiles over a straw skirt **(69)**. Standing on the back of one animal masquerade was a small *maani* puppet wearing a traditional Fulani hat. The head of the other *Sogo bò* puppet masquerade was difficult to specifically identify at a distance but might have been a giraffe or camel. Two standing *maani* figures performed on its back.

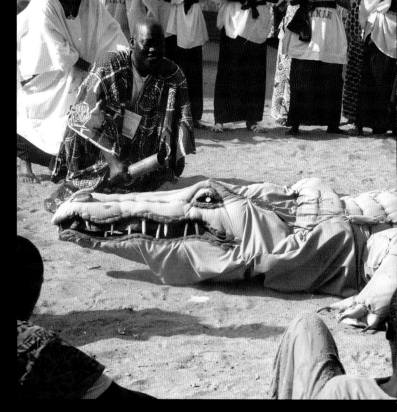

65. **Bala**, the porcupine, is a Boso puppet masquerade made entirely of grass. Note the lead singer (left) with a microphone, the chorus of women clapping hands, and the attendant with a bell (right). Ségou, Mali, 2008.

66. **Bama**, the crocodile, appears as a Boso cloth puppet masquerade. The lead attendant on the left is using a bell to guide the crocodile while a second attendant on the right speaks to the animal. Ségou, Mali, 2008.

67. The lead attendant in a white outfit is speaking to **Sa**, the snake, in the form of a Boso cloth puppet masquerade. A bell in the attendant's left hand is hidden by the snake's body. A man on the right is prodding the snake with a pole. Ségou, Mali, 2008.

68. The snake responds to the prodding by raising its head and tail at the same time. Ségou, Mali, 2008.

69. Boso animal puppet masquerades are carried in pirogues on the Niger River. Attendants are seated and standing next to the masquerades. The audience in the foreground is on the beach. Ségou, Mali, 2008.

Wulujègè, the dogfish, was carried in a pirogue before it was launched into the water. It had a mouth full of pointed teeth and a body sheathed in silvery, painted plastic sheeting **(70)**. Until the moment it slid from the pirogue into the water, the fish puppet was hidden from view by a blue plastic tarp. Movement of the fish in the shallow water was produced by a person crouching inside who was directed by signals from a bell-wielding attendant wading nearby.

After the puppet performances had concluded, we paid a visit to the nearby village of Ségoukoro (Sékoro). Ségoukoro and Ségou were centers of the Bambara kingdom led at its height by Bitòn Mamary Coulibaly in the 18th century. He is represented among our puppets as a horseman **(Sotogi)** in traditional Bamana garb holding a sword in his outstretched arm. A woman, said to be his wife, is mounted behind him. The once important town of Ségoukoro, built on a slope that descends to the shore of the Niger River, has now become a quiet village in the outskirts of Ségou. Here we were greeted by a small army of friendly children who clutched our hands. Under the direction of one of the village "guides", this lively group escorted us to see the sights, including the well-maintained gravesite of Bitòn Coulibaly **(71)**.

70

71

70. *Wulujègè*, the dogfish, a Boso puppet masquerade of shiny plastic stretched over an armature, is moving in the Niger River next to the pirogue from which it was launched. Ségou, Mali, 2008.

71. The gravesite of Biton Coulibaly in Ségoukoro, Mali, 2008.

By chance near the sandy shore of the river, we came upon two women pounding millet in a mortar **(72)**. In addition to children, the women were attended by several chickens that busily scurried about to capture each particle of grain that fell from the mortar. This domestic scene is duplicated by a puppet included in this volume showing women pounding millet *(Nyò-susu-musow)*. One of the women allowed Sue Rosen to test her skill at pounding, much to the amusement of the children **(73)**.

72. Two women pounding millet in the shade of a tree near the Niger River in Ségoukoro, Mali, 2008.

73. Mary Sue Rosen takes a turn at pounding millet in Ségoukoro, Mali, 2008.

74 A, B

CHAPTER SIX

SOGO BÒ CHARACTERS AND THEMES

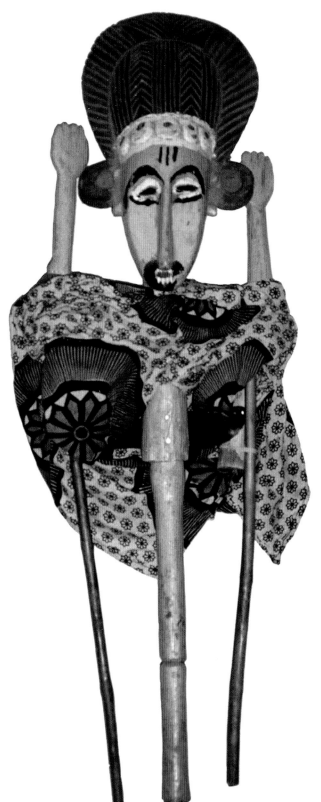

Some *Sogo bò* characters reflect the core identity of the ethnic group responsible for the performance. Farming themes, animals of the bush, and bush spirits dominate performances of the Bamana and Maraka people whose livelihood depends on farming or trading and in the past also relied on hunting. On the other hand, performances of the Sòmonò and Boso groups who rely on fishing are more concerned with characters and animals associated with the water, in particular those found in the nearby the Niger River. Farmers present animals such as elephants, lions, antelope, agricultural activities such as hoeing and winnowing grain, as well as warriors, and hunters. Fishermen perform crocodiles, fish, hippos and men in pirogues, the traditional Niger River boats.

Other characters are shared by farmers and fishermen, including some "little people" or *maani*, bush spirits, birds, antelope, and wildcats.

An important set of themes revolves around women, including marriage, polygamy, children, adultery, and divorce. Social and contemporary issues such as fashion, politics, illiteracy, gender equality or lack thereof, management of finances, and the control of AIDS may also be addressed. Animals are a means for discussing admirable human qualities and human faults in metaphorical terms. The cultural identity of the community is reaffirmed as a consequence of these annual festivals by assuring the transmission of the community's rich oral literature, traditions, and collective imagination to the next generation. Coincidentally, the events serve as a means for modifying traditions to achieve changes in social behavior that are perceived to be beneficial to the community.

Masks, puppets, and puppet masquerades of the Malian *Sogo bò* theatre can be grouped into several broad categories according to the topics, circumstances and events that they depict: village life; heroic and important men; wild animals; spirits of the bush; and beautiful women. These sometimes overlapping categories representing aspects of Malian life and beliefs provide a contextual framework for understanding the range of subjects and characters embodied by *Sogo bò* performances.

VILLAGE LIFE

This theme encompasses many of the important subjects addressed in *Sogo bò* theatre. These performances, generally enacted by masked figures or small, articulated puppets who appear on the head or back of a *sogoba* masquerade, provide an opportunity to comment on the roles played by various characters in the village's social life, the interactions of youth and their elders, daily family and communal activities, as well as past, present, and future events. Many rod puppets in the collection illustrate this theme. They include: female figures (74-78), figures representing a man or an elder man whose beard is a sign of wisdom *(Cèkòròba)* (79-85), village couples (86-88), a farmer *(Cikèla)* with a hoe (20, 89-91), a farmer *(Cikèla)* with his plow and oxen (21, 92), a woman carding cotton *(Koorishena- muso)* (93), women winnowing grain *(Nyò-surulan-musow)*, (91, 94), women pounding grain *(Nyò-susu-musow)* (55, 72, 95, 96), and Boso fishermen in a boat (97).

75 A, B, C

74 A, B. This is a rod puppet female figure with a finely carved coiffure and pigmentation around her mouth that represents indigo tattooing. The arms are moved by sticks attached to them near the shoulders. H 36.5 in. Wood, cloth, paint.

75 A, B, C. A Janus head female figure with arms articulated at the shoulders. She has henna designs on her hands, indigo tattooing on her lower lip, cowrie shell earrings, and painted necklaces. These features and the traditional *kunwililen* hairstyle suggest that she is probably a young bride. This puppet was worn on top of the head since the body has a cup-shaped base and handles for attachment. H 29 in. Wood, paint, cowrie shells.

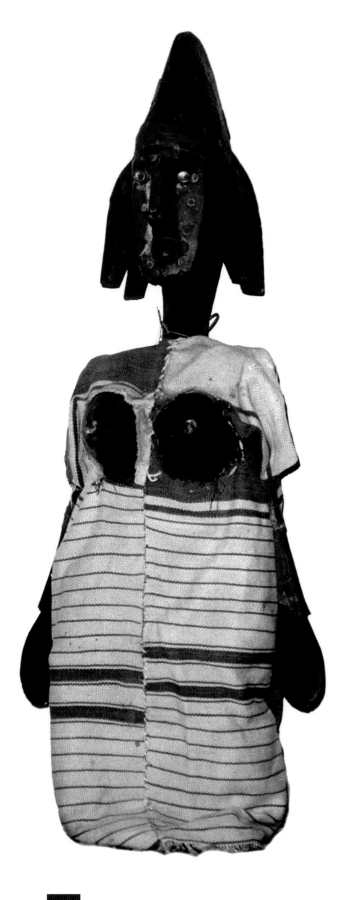

76

77

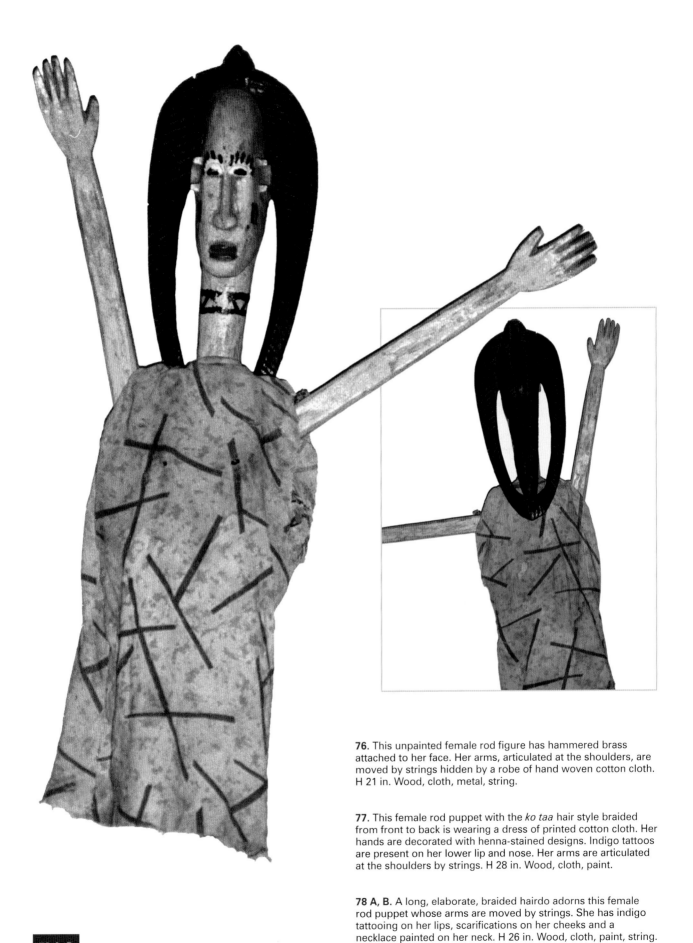

78 A, B

76. This unpainted female rod figure has hammered brass attached to her face. Her arms, articulated at the shoulders, are moved by strings hidden by a robe of hand woven cotton cloth. H 21 in. Wood, cloth, metal, string.

77. This female rod puppet with the *ko taa* hair style braided from front to back is wearing a dress of printed cotton cloth. Her hands are decorated with henna-stained designs. Indigo tattoos are present on her lower lip and nose. Her arms are articulated at the shoulders by strings. H 28 in. Wood, cloth, paint.

78 A, B. A long, elaborate, braided hairdo adorns this female rod puppet whose arms are moved by strings. She has indigo tattooing on her lips, scarifications on her cheeks and a necklace painted on her neck. H 26 in. Wood, cloth, paint, string.

79 A, B

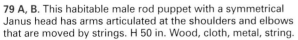

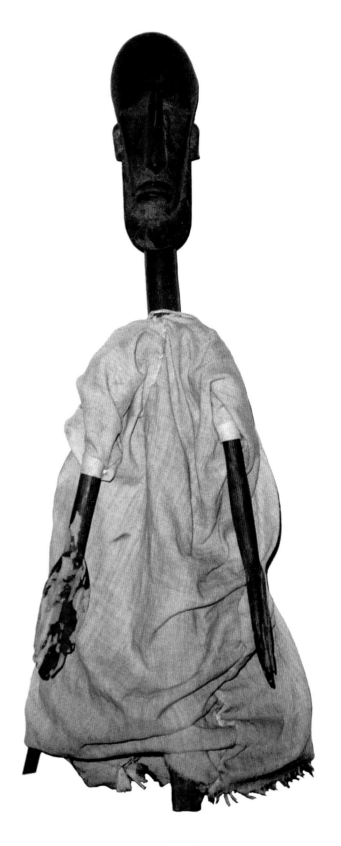

79 A, B. This habitable male rod puppet with a symmetrical Janus head has arms articulated at the shoulders and elbows that are moved by strings. H 50 in. Wood, cloth, metal, string.

80. *Cèkòròba*, an elder man wearing a blue cap and a kaftan, is a rod puppet with arms articulated at the shoulders that are moved by sticks. Insect damage is evident on one of his spoon-shaped hands. H 31.5 in. Wood, cloth, paint, metal.

81. This rod puppet of a bearded elder man, *Cèkòròba*, has a shaved head. Beneath the kaftan are sticks that manipulate the arms at the shoulders. Insect damage is apparent on the right arm and hand. H 32 in. Wood, paint, cloth, metal.

82. *Cèkòròba,* a bearded elder man with painted facial scarifications, wears a small, round cap. The rod puppet's arms are articulated at the shoulders and moved by strings. H 27 in. Wood, cloth, paint, string.

83. This bearded elder male *Cèkòròba* rod puppet is wearing a blue cap and a printed cotton kaftan. The arms are articulated at the shoulders by strings. H 25.5 in. Wood, cloth, paint, string.

84. A bearded elder man, *Cèkòròba,* with a white cap in the form of a body puppet. The puppet's arms were attached separately, possibly to the figure's cloth costume, and it extended above the performer's head. H 37.5 in. Wood, paint.

85. This habitable body puppet of a bearded elder man, *Cèkòròba,* was obtained from Yaya Coulibaly in 2003. The arms are manipulated by rods. H 39 in. Wood, cloth, paint.

86 A, B

87 A, B

86. A, B. A bearded elder man, *Cèkòròba*, and his wife are rod puppets that wear robes made of hand woven cotton cloth. The woman has the *ko taa* hairstyle and earrings. Strings hidden by the robes move the arms that are articulated at the shoulders. A: H 27 in. Wood, cloth, paint, metal, string. B: H 26.5 in. Wood, cloth, paint, metal, string, beads, cowries.

87. A, B. A bearded elder man, *Cèkòròba*, and his wife. The man wears a yellow cap and a robe made from hand woven cotton cloth. The woman's robe is made from printed cotton cloth, and she wears earrings. The arms of both figures are moved by strings and they both have forehead scarifications. A: H 25.5 in. Wood, cloth, paint, metal, string. B: H 26.5 in. Wood, cloth, paint, metal, string, beads, cowries.

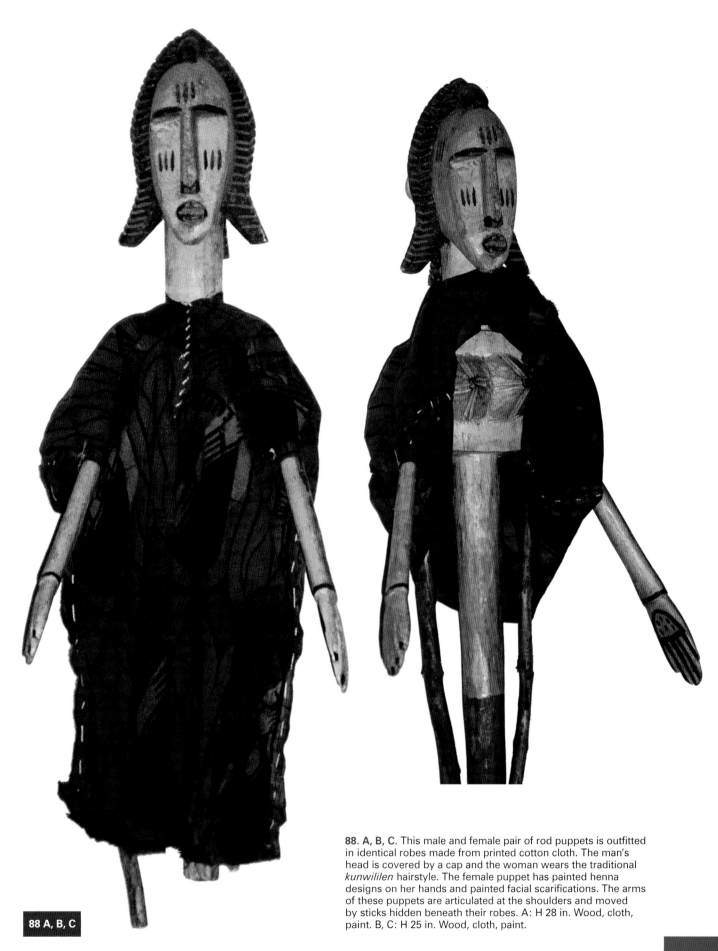

88 A, B, C

88. A, B, C. This male and female pair of rod puppets is outfitted in identical robes made from printed cotton cloth. The man's head is covered by a cap and the woman wears the traditional *kunwililen* hairstyle. The female puppet has painted henna designs on her hands and painted facial scarifications. The arms of these puppets are articulated at the shoulders and moved by sticks hidden beneath their robes. A: H 28 in. Wood, cloth, paint. B, C: H 25 in. Wood, cloth, paint.

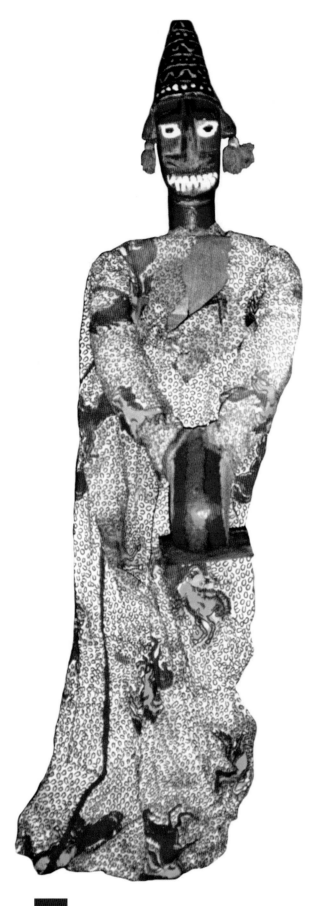

89

90

89. Cikèla, the farmer, is a rod puppet whose arms, articulated at the shoulders, move together to raise and lower a hoe (*daba*). The farmer's cap is painted with a mud cloth (*bogolan*) design. H 27 in. Wood, cloth, paint, metal.

90. This rod puppet head of **Dajè**, the roan antelope, carries a puppet figure representing a farmer, ***Cikèla***, with a hoe (*daba*). The farmer's arms are articulated and are moved from below by a string. The antelope's jaw is articulated and held in place by a rubber strap. H 36 in. Wood, paint, cloth, metal, string, rubber.

91 A, B, C. *Sigi*, the buffalo, carries articulated figures on its back, consisting of an upper pair of farmers wielding hoes, a lower pair of women winnowing grain, and a crocodile. Strings that run behind ***Sigi***'s back raise and lower the farmers' hoes and the winnowers' trays as well as the head and tail of the crocodile that are attached to its body by cloth sleeves. ***Sigi***'s second white set of horns was added for dramatic effect. His lower jaw, held in place by a rubber strap, is moved by a string. H 40 in. Wood, paint, cloth, string, rubber.

91 A, B, C

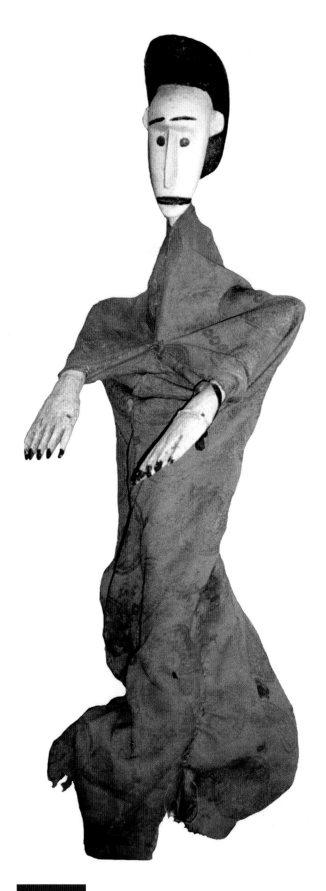

92 A, B, C, D

92. A, B, C, D. *Cikèla*, the farmer, stands with his arms outstretched to hold a plow. Metal rods hidden by the farmer's robe move his arms. Red paint has been applied to his fingernails for dramatic effect. The plow resembles those found at the iron recycling market in Bamako. A team of hump back oxen with a yoke and chain pulls the plow.
A: H 29.5 in. Wood, cloth, paint, metal, rubber. B: H 25 in. Wood, paint, metal rubber. C: H 15 in. Wood, paint, metal, fiber.

93

94

95

93. A rod puppet representing a woman carding cotton, ***Koorishena-muso***, stands on a wooden platform. Her arms that move apart are articulated at the shoulders by metal rods. She wears a printed cotton robe and has an earring. H 29 in. Wood, cloth, metal, paint, plant fiber.

94. The rod puppet head of ***Dajè***, the roan antelope, is surmounted by a female figure winnowing grain (***Nyò-surulan-muso***). The woman's arms holding a winnowing tray are articulated at the shoulders and moved by string from below. A string moves ***Dajè's*** jaw that is held in place by a rubber strap. H 40 in. Wood, paint, cloth, metal, string, rubber.

95. Two women pounding grain (***Nyò susu-musow***) are represented by articulated female puppets attached to a wooden platform. The women's arms can be raised and lowered to simulate pounding in the mortar. The birds are picking up spilt grain. H 28 in. Wood, paint, cloth, metal.

96

96. This antelope rod puppet, possibly ***Dajè***, the roan antelope, has a woman pounding grain (***Nyò-susu-muso***) seated between its horns. The woman's arms, articulated at the shoulders, are moved from below by strings. H 28 in. Wood, paint, cloth, string.

97. The articulated limbs of the rod puppet Boso fishermen in a pirogue are moved from below by strings. H 17.5 in. Wood, paint, cloth, metal, string.

97

Important domesticated animals represented by rod puppet heads are *Misi,* the Zebu cattle, a symbol of prosperity or abundance (22, 98-102), *Bakòrò,* the ram, a symbol of wisdom and maturity (49, 103-106), *So,* the horse, a beloved and honored animal that is a symbol of wealth and prestige (51,107), and the donkey (108).

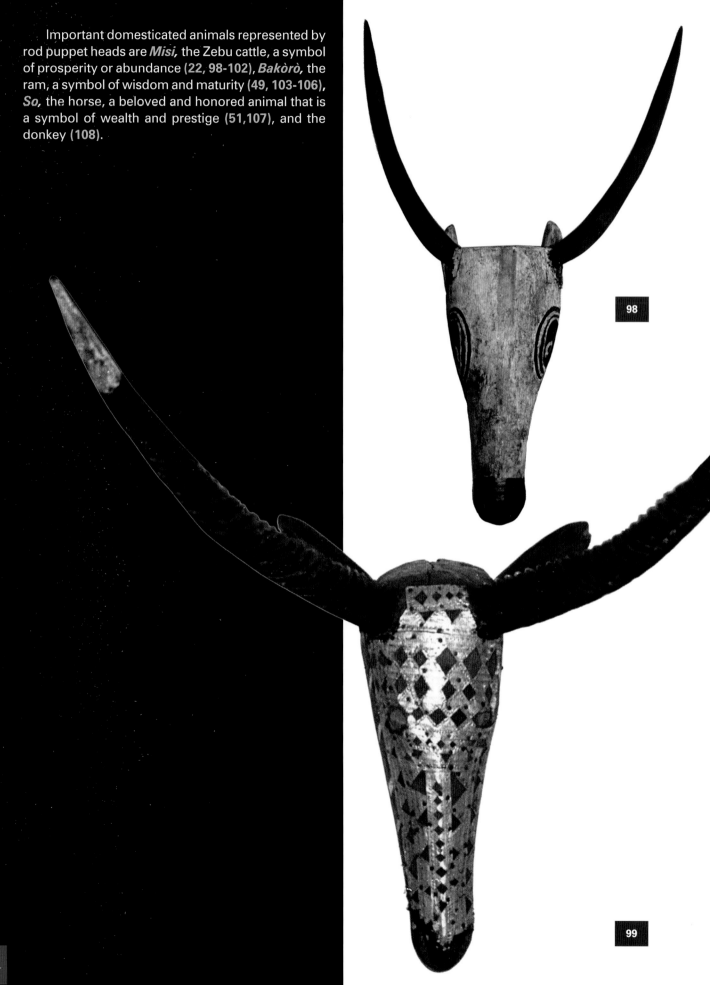

98

99

98. *Misi*, the zebu cow puppet head, has long, sweeping horns and an articulated lower jaw that is held in place by a rubber strap. H 48 in. Wood, paint, metal, rubber.

99. *Misi*, the zebu cow puppet head, is decorated with cut metal appliqué. H 24.5 in. Wood, paint, metal.

100. The puppet head of a zebu bull has a ring through its nose. H 38 in. Wood, paint, metal.

101. *Misi*, the zebu cow puppet head, has a crescent moon painted on her forehead that may be an Islamic motif. The horns are hinged and articulated. H 30 in. Wood, paint, metal.

100

101

102

103

104

102. *Misi,* the zebu cow puppet head, has long, elegant horns. A man seated between the horns may be a village chief wearing a pith helmet as a symbol of status, or he could be a colonial figure. His arms and legs, articulated at the shoulders and hips, are moved from below by strings. The horns and head are painted with elaborate, geometric designs. Remnants of small sticks that protruded along the length of the horns are present. H 67 in. Wood, paint, cloth, metal, string.

103. This rod puppet head of *Bakòrò,* the ram, has a sleeve of printed cotton cloth covering the handle. The articulated ears are moved from below by strings. H 17 in. Wood, cloth, paint, metal, string.

104. This blue rod puppet head of *Bakòrò,* the ram, has no moving parts. H 14.5 in. Wood, paint.

105. The articulated lower jaw of this rod puppet head of *Bakòrò,* the ram, is held in place by a rubber strap. The sleeve covering the handle is made from the same cloth as the robe on the female rod puppet in Figure **87 B.** H 13.5 in. Wood, cloth, paint, metal, rubber.

105

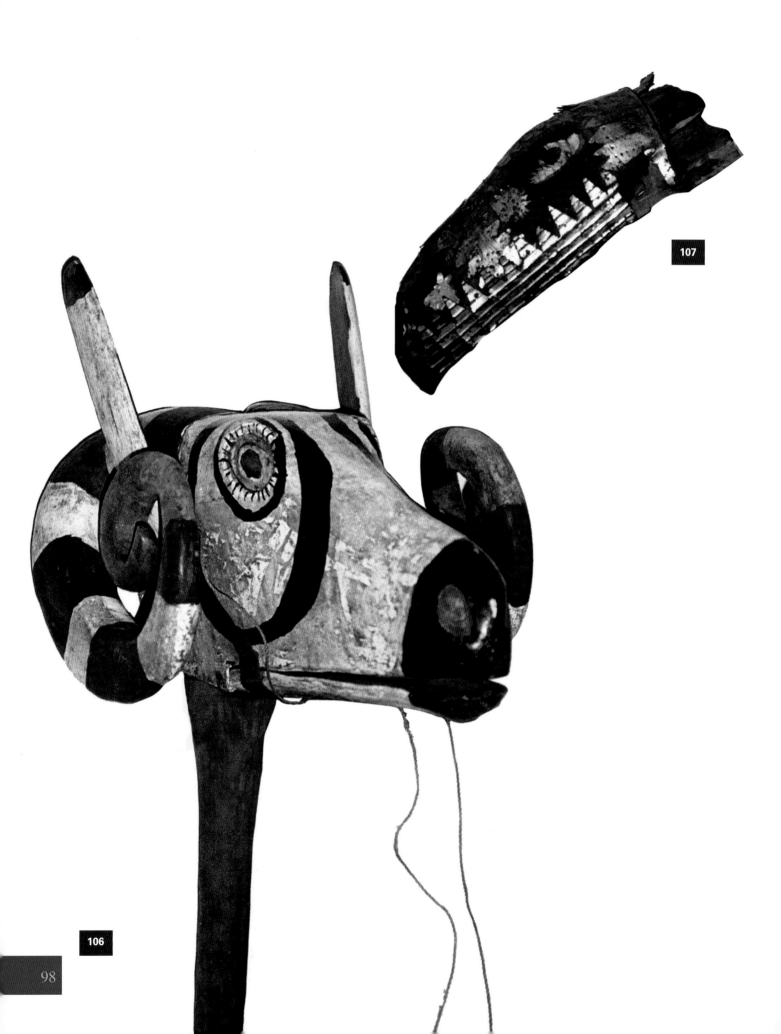

108

106. The ridges on the horns of this rod puppet head of **Bakòrò**, the ram, are painted rather than carved. The handle is visible as are strings used to move the ears and lower jaw. H 23.5 in. Wood, paint, metal, rubber, string.

107. This unusually heavy puppet head depicts **Sa**, the horse. It is embellished with metal and cloth appliqué. Eyelashes fashioned from cloth surround the eyes. H 25 in. Wood, cloth, metal, paint.

108. This rod puppet head may represent a donkey. The articulated lower jaw is held in place by a rubber strap, and there is a red cloth sleeve. H 13 in. Wood, cloth, paint, metal, rubber.

Human characters are sometimes represented in combination with animals of the bush. This is exemplified by puppets of *Dajè*, the roan antelope and *Sigi*, the buffalo, that are surmounted by human puppet characters. These include mothers with their children seated on *Sigi* (109), three figures seated on *Sigi*, possibly a parent and children (110), a woman pounding grain who is seated on *Dajè* (96), a farmer hoeing seated on *Dajè* (90), a woman winnowing grain seated on *Dajè* (94), and women winnowing grain seated on *Sigi* (91). The conjunction of these animal and human characters is consistent with the belief of the Bamana people that they learned the art of farming from *Dajè*, the roan antelope. *Ciwara,* a stylized form of *Dajè* that usually appears as a head crest mask at agricultural festivals, is sometimes carved on the horns of a roan antelope rod puppet head (111-113) or on the horns of *Sigi* (114).

109 A, B, C

100

109. A, B, C. *Sigi*, the buffalo, supports three articulated female figures. A woman is seated between *Sigi*'s horns. The figures on top of the horns have the shaved hairstyle that was traditionally worn by children. The arms and legs of the figures are moved by strings. *Sigi*'s articulated lower jaw is held in place by a rubber strap. Strings to the upper figures run along the backs of the horns. H 42.5 in. Wood, paint, cloth, string, metal, rubber.

110 A, B, C

110. A, B, C. A female figure is seated on the crown of *Sigi*'s head, and there is a male figure at the top of each horn. The arms and legs of the figures are moved by strings, and *Sigi*'s articulated lower jaw is held in place by a rubber strap. Strings to the upper figures run along the backs of the horns. H 49 in. Wood, paint, cloth, metal, string, rubber.

111. The horns of this puppet head of *Dajè*, the roan antelope, are carved to represent *Ciwara*, a mythical roan antelope. Strings move the female puppet's articulated limbs from below. The antelope's moveable lower jaw is held in place by a rubber strap. H 35 in. Wood, paint, cloth, string, metal, rubber.

112. This rod puppet head of *Dajè*, the roan antelope, has horns carved in the form of *Ciwara*, a mythical roan antelope. The articulated arms of the female figure on *Dajè*'s forehead are moved by strings hidden by the cloth sleeve that covers the wooden rod handle. H 30.5 in. Wood, paint, cloth, metal.

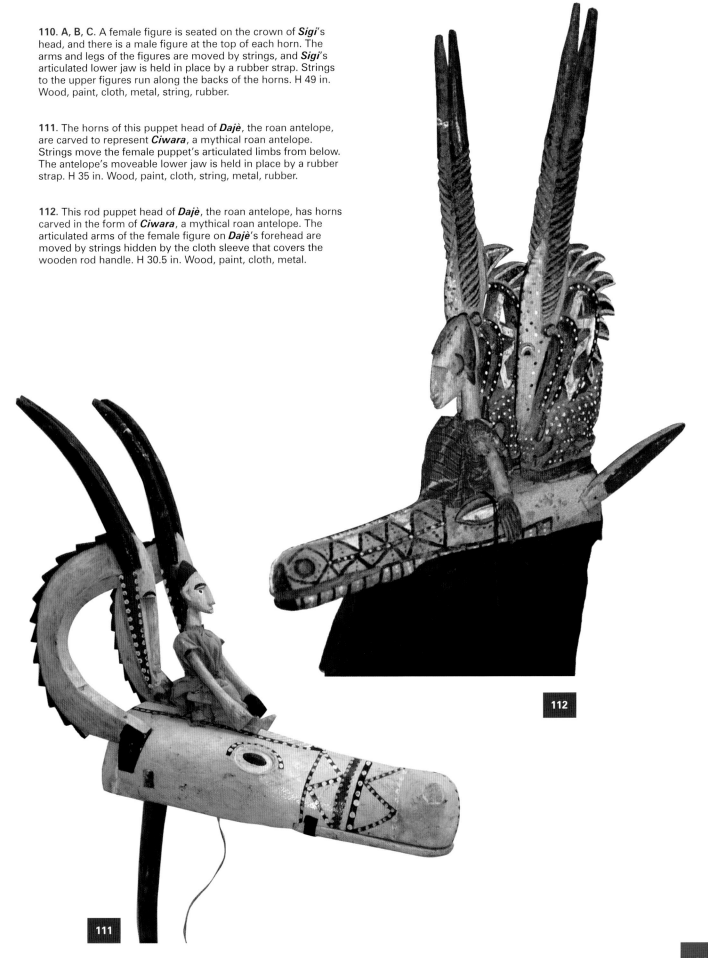

112

111

103

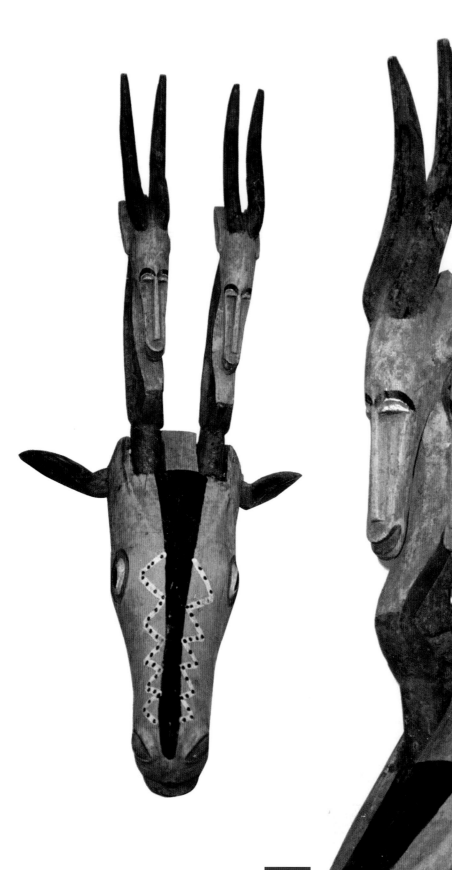

113 A, B

113. A, B. Ciwara, the mythical roan antelope of the Bamana people, appears on the horns of this antelope rod puppet head, possibly representing *Dajè*, the roan antelope. H 26 in. Wood, paint, metal.

114. A, B. The horns of *Sigi*, the buffalo, carry the mythical roan antelope, *Ciwara*, on this puppet head. A rubber strap holds the articulated jaw in place. H 35 in. Wood, paint, rubber, metal.

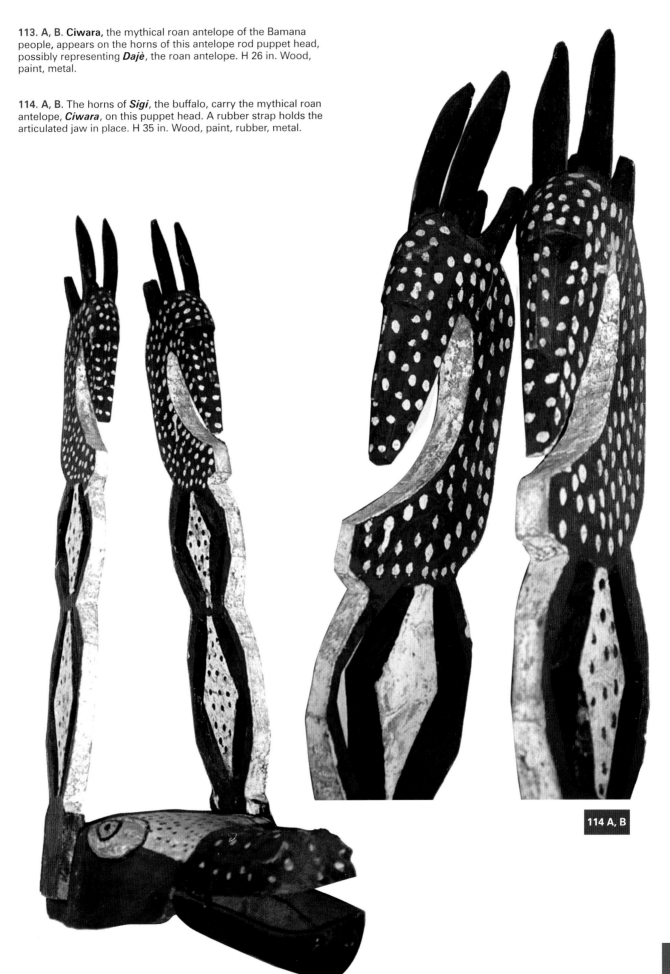

114 A, B

105

The *Kòrèduga* is a special type of rod puppet. It consists of a wooden rod with a horse head carved at one end or a carved horse head with a socket into which a rod is inserted (115). The midportion of the rod may be carved to represent a saddle. The face of the horse is often embellished with brass appliqué. Horsehair is sometimes attached to the neck to represent a mane and at the rear of the rod for a tail (116, 117). *Kòrèduga* puppets are used by men during initiation into the *Kòrè* society who place the rod between their legs and perform a dance in which they mimic riding a horse.

During public events such as *Sogo bò* theatre, men and women acting as *Kòrèduga* clowns are dressed in cloth outfits to which an odd assortment of discarded junk objects are attached (32). The women shake rattles, and the men perform with musical instruments that are sometimes improvised from junk material. Men carrying wooden swords or other objects dance astride *Kòrèduga* horse puppets (31). They satirize customs in need of change and mock public figures in positions of authority (village elders, chiefs, or government administrators) and classes of people who derive power from special knowledge (warriors, hunters or Islamic scholars, the marabouts). The purpose of the performance is to promote social values and morality by making fun of hypocrisy and irresponsible behavior.

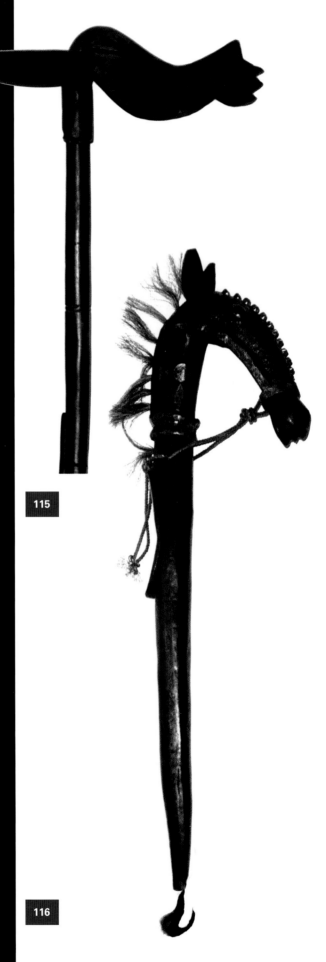

115

116

115. A rod fits into the socket in the neck of this *Kòrèduga* horse rod puppet. H 23.5 in. Wood, pigment.

116. Brass appliqué has been attached to the face and neck of this *Kòrèduga* rod puppet that was carved from a single piece of wood. The horses mane and tail are made of hair. A saddle has been carved on the rod. H 34 in. Wood, brass, hair, rope.

117. A, B. This *Kòrèduga* horse rod puppet carved from a single piece of wood has brass applique on its face, a mane and tail of hair, and a saddle. Mild insect damage is present. H 36 in. Wood, brass, hair, rope.

117 A, B

A heroic or important man may be a Bamana historical figure and warrior such as Biton Coulibaly, the founder of the pre-colonial Segou empire (71,118), a Tuareg warrior on a camel (119), a champion farmer (90), *Sotigi,* a horseman (120), a government officer (121), a marabout (122), or a hunter who has conquered the dangerous animals and spirits of the bush (123).

Hunters form a powerful society whose members are the keepers of secret knowledge about the nature of animals, the medicinal properties of plants, and magical incantations that allow them to perform miracles. In Bamana oral history, hunters are credited with having founded many villages that formed the Mali Empire. Hunters have several important roles in *Sogo bò* puppet theatre, and they are celebrated in songs that accompany certain puppets and masquerades such as *Sigi,* the buffalo (124). They appear as small puppets on the backs of masquerades and in some scenes, they hunt wild animals such as *Waraba,* the lion, represented by a masked performer.

The successful hunter or fisherman acquires heroic status through deeds that are recounted in the puppet performance. Masquerades involving wild animals sometimes speak to the competition between youthful members of the community (hunters as agents for change) and their elders (bound by tradition) as young men seek to exceed the accomplishments of prior generations and to forge a new reality. In the contemporary context, hunting themed masquerades may be metaphors for young men (hunters or fishermen) who have ventured away from their home village to support their families by finding employment in Bamako, the capital of Mali, or in a foreign country (symbolized by the bush or water inhabited by dangerous animals and spirits).

118 A, B

118. A, B. The horseman, *Sotigi*, on this large, multipart puppet is said to be Biton Coulibaly, the founder of the Ségou empire in the early 18th century, with his wife. The articulated limbs of both figures are moved from below by strings. The figures, as well as the horse's head and the tail, can be detached from the horse's body. H 38 in. Wood, cloth, paint, string, metal.

119. The figure seated on the back of a camel, **Nyaamè,** was identified as a warrior of the Tuareg people who live in the desert region of northern Mali. The man's arms and legs are moved by strings from below. H 29.5 in. Wood, paint, cloth, string.

119

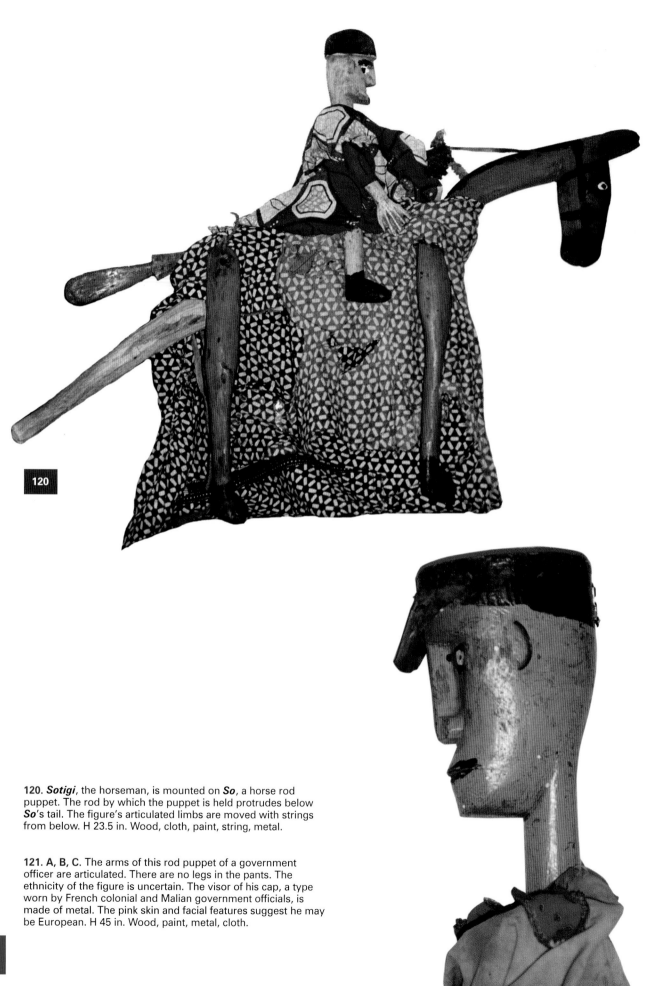

120. *Sotigi*, the horseman, is mounted on ***So***, a horse rod puppet. The rod by which the puppet is held protrudes below ***So***'s tail. The figure's articulated limbs are moved with strings from below. H 23.5 in. Wood, cloth, paint, string, metal.

121. A, B, C. The arms of this rod puppet of a government officer are articulated. There are no legs in the pants. The ethnicity of the figure is uncertain. The visor of his cap, a type worn by French colonial and Malian government officials, is made of metal. The pink skin and facial features suggest he may be European. H 45 in. Wood, paint, metal, cloth.

121 A, B, C

122. This rod puppet figure of **Morikè**, a marabout, has arms articulated at the shoulders that are moved by sticks hidden by his caftan. H 29.5 in. Wood, paint, cloth.

123. **A, B**. **Sigi**, the buffalo, carries a pair of hunters with rifles (below) and a pair of women winnowing grain (above) on his back. These figures, as well as the crocodile's head and tail, and **Sigi**'s ears and jaw, are moved by strings. The crocodile's head and tail are connected to its body by cloth sleeves. A second set of white horns has been added for dramatic effect. H 40 in. Wood, paint, cloth, string, metal, rubber.

124. This elegant rod puppet head of **Sigi**, the buffalo, has long, string whiskers hanging from its articulated jaw that is held in place by a rubber strap. The color and design painted on **Sigi** are complemented by the printed cotton cloth sleeve. H 24.5 in. Wood, paint, cloth, rubber, string, metal.

124

WILD ANIMALS

The animal characters were among the earliest puppet forms, and they still play an important role in *Sogo bò* puppet theatre. Representing the dangerous realm of the wilderness and water that men must master as hunters or fishermen, the animal characters are symbols and metaphors for the behavior of men as traditional providers for their families and communities.

Sigi is one of the most frequently represented bush animals in Bamana puppet masquerades. **Sigi** usually appears as a rod puppet head with one or more small articulated **maani** puppets on the crown of its head and on its horns or as a puppet masquerade with puppets on its back (**91, 109, 110, 123, 124**). **Sigi** also appears with **Ciwara** (**114**) or birds (**125**) on its horns. The savage, brute strength and unpredictable temper of the male buffalo make it a dangerous prey for hunters. It serves as a metaphor for the virility and untamed power of young men. The juxtaposition of human characters with a dangerous bush animal suggests man's ability to conquer the bush and the unknown.

125 A, B

125. A, B. *Sigi*, a buffalo, carries a crocodile on his forehead and birds on his horns. The articulated head and tail of the crocodile, attached to its body by cloth sleeves, are moved by strings from below. The hinged ears flap with the puppet's motion and the articulated jaw is held in place by a rubber strap. H 10 in. Wood, paint, cloth, string, rubber, metal.

Waraba, the lion (53, 126, 127), is an important bush animal for the Bamana people because it's power and ability as a hunter make it particularly dangerous to approach and subdue. It may also refer to political authority that can be overthrown if it abuses its powers.

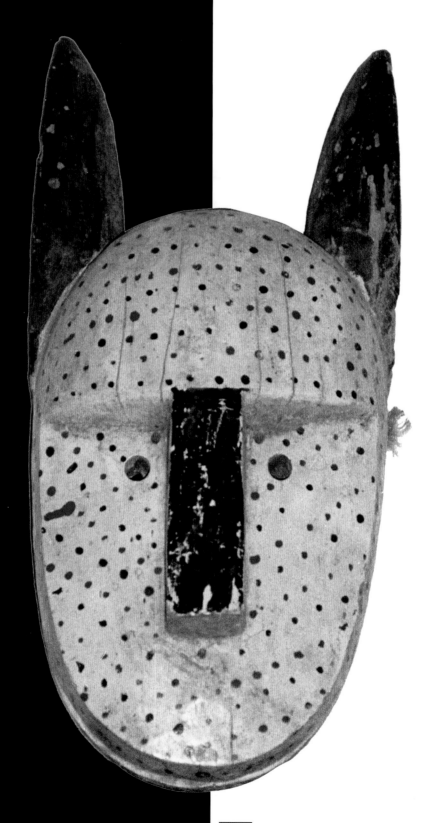

126

126. The mask of *Waraba*, the lion, has painted red and black spots. H 16.5 in. Wood, paint.

127. A, B. This unusual mask of *Waraba*, the lion, is decorated with designs painted on paper that has been glued to the wooden mask. The articulated jaw is held in place by string. This mask was identified as belonging to the Boso people. H 20 in. Wood, paint, paper, string.

Nama, the hyena, **(50, 128, 129),** a skillful hunter known for its intelligence and endurance, is a symbol of the community elders. It is thought to possess great knowledge that allows it to predict good and bad events. In some performances it assumes a religious or mystical role.

128. As a rod puppet, ***Nama,*** the hyena, displays impressive teeth that make him a successful hunter. His eyes are bright metal tacks. A rubber strap holds the articulated jaw in place. H 29 in. Wood, paint, metal, string, rubber.

129. A mask of **Nama,** the hyena. H 12.5 in. Wood, paint.

128

Other dangerous animals in the bush that challenge the hunter are *Jè,* the warthog (**130**), *Sama,* the elephant (**57, 131, 132**), and *Waraninkalan,* the panther (**133**). In various contexts, all of the dangerous animals of the bush symbolize the challenges that men have to overcome in order to achieve heroic stature by acquiring the life force of the prey that has been subdued.

130

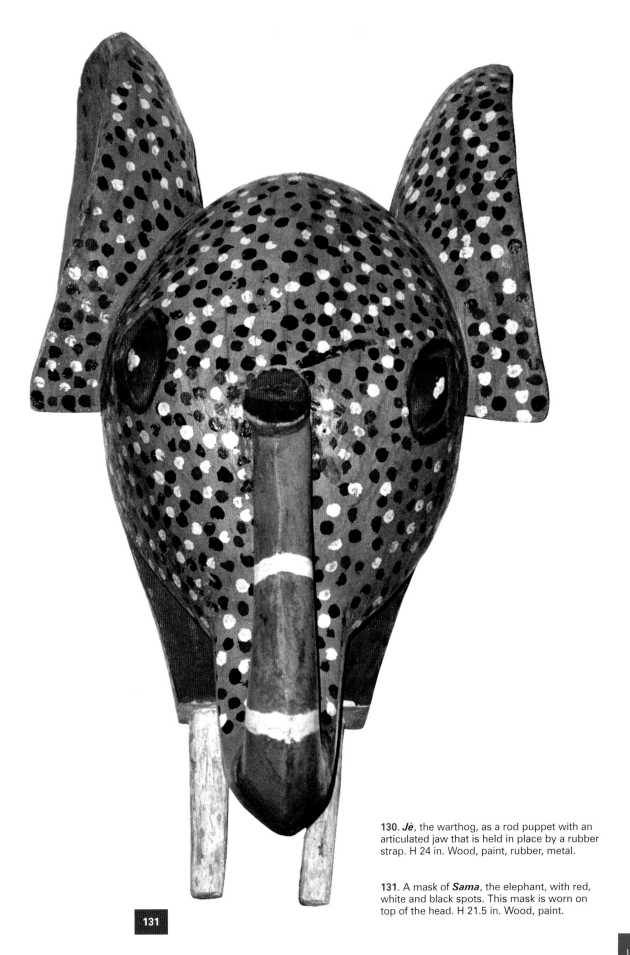

131

130. *Jè*, the warthog, as a rod puppet with an articulated jaw that is held in place by a rubber strap. H 24 in. Wood, paint, rubber, metal.

131. A mask of **Sama**, the elephant, with red, white and black spots. This mask is worn on top of the head. H 21.5 in. Wood, paint.

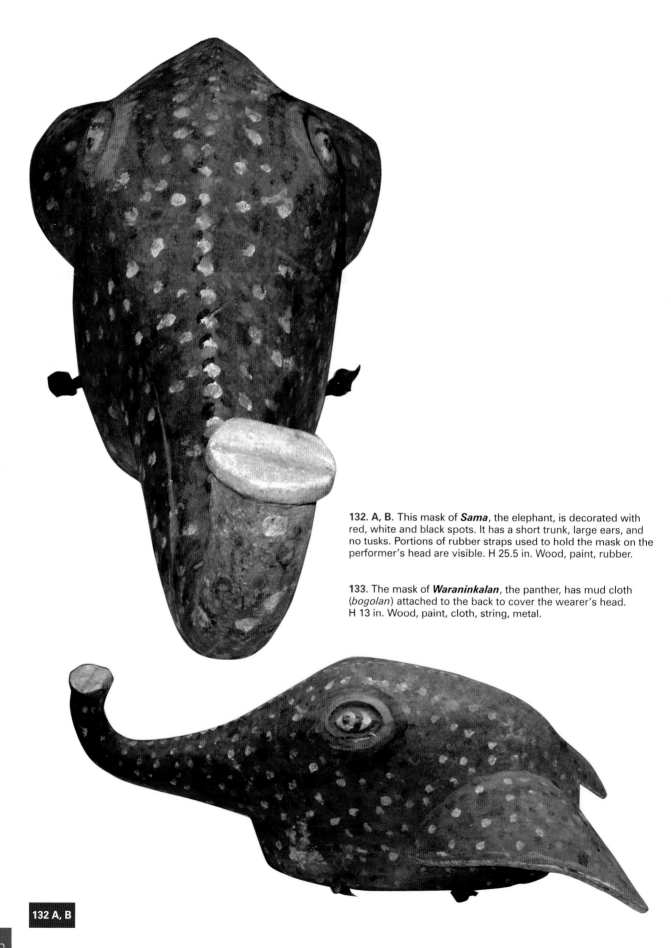

132. A, B. This mask of **Sama**, the elephant, is decorated with red, white and black spots. It has a short trunk, large ears, and no tusks. Portions of rubber straps used to hold the mask on the performer's head are visible. H 25.5 in. Wood, paint, rubber.

133. The mask of **Waraninkalan**, the panther, has mud cloth (*bogolan*) attached to the back to cover the wearer's head. H 13 in. Wood, paint, cloth, string, metal.

132 A, B

As denizens of the bush and important prey for hunters, several types of antelope that appear in *Sogo bò* puppet theatre are represented in the collection. Among those not illustrated in the foregoing pages are additional examples of *Dajè*, the roan antelope (134, 135), several antelope that might be **Dajè** (136-138), **Nkòkunan,** the duiker antelope (139), **Sensen,** the waterbuck (140), **Sine,** the gazelle (141), **Dankalankule,** the oryx (142, 143), and other unidentified antelope (144-148). The antelope is considered to be a treacherous animal because men may be seduced by its beauty and graceful movements, and its ability to tirelessly run long distances is a metaphor for perseverance and courage.

134

124

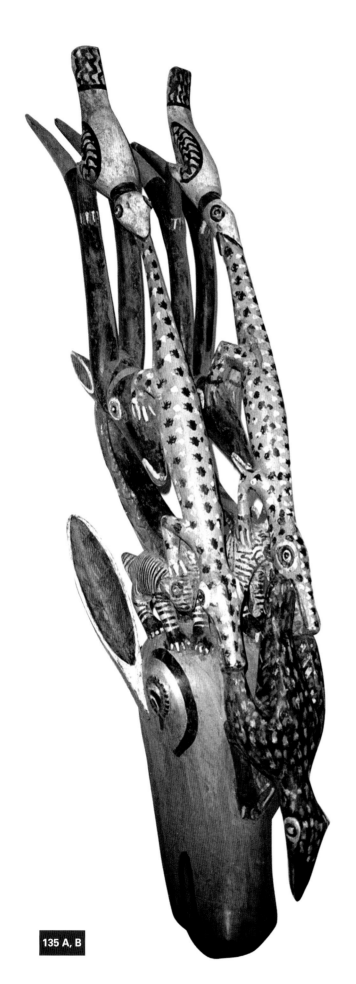

134. This is a rod puppet head of ***Dajè***, the roan antelope, with a male figure wearing a cap on the crown of its head. The articulated arms of the figure are moved from below by strings, and the articulated jaw is held in place by a rubber strap. H 21in. Wood, paint, cloth, string, rubber, metal.

135. A, B. This stunning rod puppet head of ***Dajè***, the roan antelope, carries an extraordinary menagerie of animals. The horns are carved in the form of ***Ciwara***, the mythical roan antelope. Two lizards (or crocodiles) hold a bird by its wings, and in turn smaller birds are biting the tails of the lizards. Two black and white striped animals are observing the struggle. This puppet head has no articulated parts. H 41in. Wood, paint, metal.

135 A, B

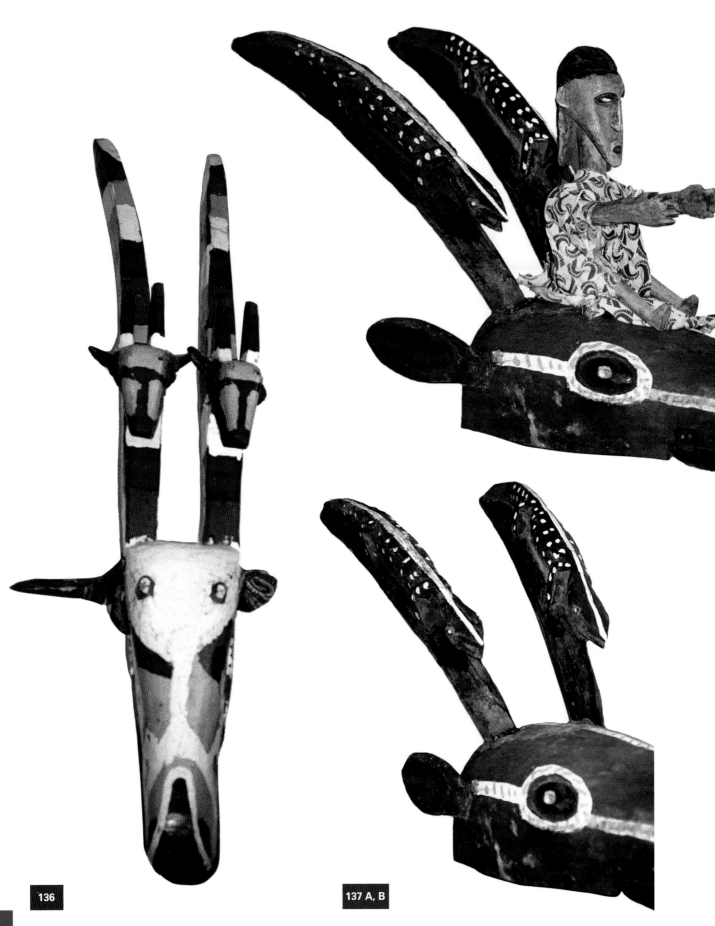

136. This rod puppet head of an antelope, possibly ***Dajè,*** the roan antelope, has secondary antelope heads on its horns. The articulated ears of the large and small antelope heads are attached to the horns by cloth sleeves and moved by strings from below. The antelope's left ear is missing. H 40 in. Wood, paint, cloth, string, metal.

137. A, B. A man with articulated limbs and a cap is seated on the crown of this rod antelope puppet head, possibly representing ***Dajè***, the roan antelope. Situated on the antelope's horns are spotted lizards that may be chameleons. The positioning of these animals on the antelope's horns is similar to that of crocodiles in Figure **55**. The antelope's articulated jaw is held in place by a rubber strap. H 25 in. Wood, paint, cloth, string, rubber, metal.

138. This antelope rod puppet head, possibly ***Dajè*** the roan antelope, has a lizard on the crown of its head and spotted lizards that may be chameleons on its horns. The position of the animals on the antelope's horns is similar to that seen in Figures **55** and **137**. The antelope's articulated jaw is held in place by a rubber strap. H 14 in. Wood, paint, rubber, metal, string.

138

139

140

139. The rod puppet head of **Nkòkunan**, the duiker antelope, has elaborate painted decorations that include the national colors of Mali, green, yellow, and red. This puppet was obtained from Yaya Coulibaly in 2003. H 16 in. Wood, paint, metal.

140. This rod puppet head, possibly representing **Sensen**, the waterbuck antelope, has cut metal appliqué on its face. Part of a red cloth sleeve that covered the handle is visible. The articulated jaw is held in place by a rubber strap. H 30 in. Wood, paint, metal, cloth, rubber.

141. Elegant, curved horns grace this antelope rod puppet head that might be **Sine**, the gazelle. The articulated ears and jaw are moved from below by strings. H 30 in. Wood, paint, rubber, string.

142. This rod puppet head of **Dankalankule**, the oryx antelope, is decorated with red and brown cotton cloth and metal rings on its horns. H 37 in. Wood, paint, cloth, metal.

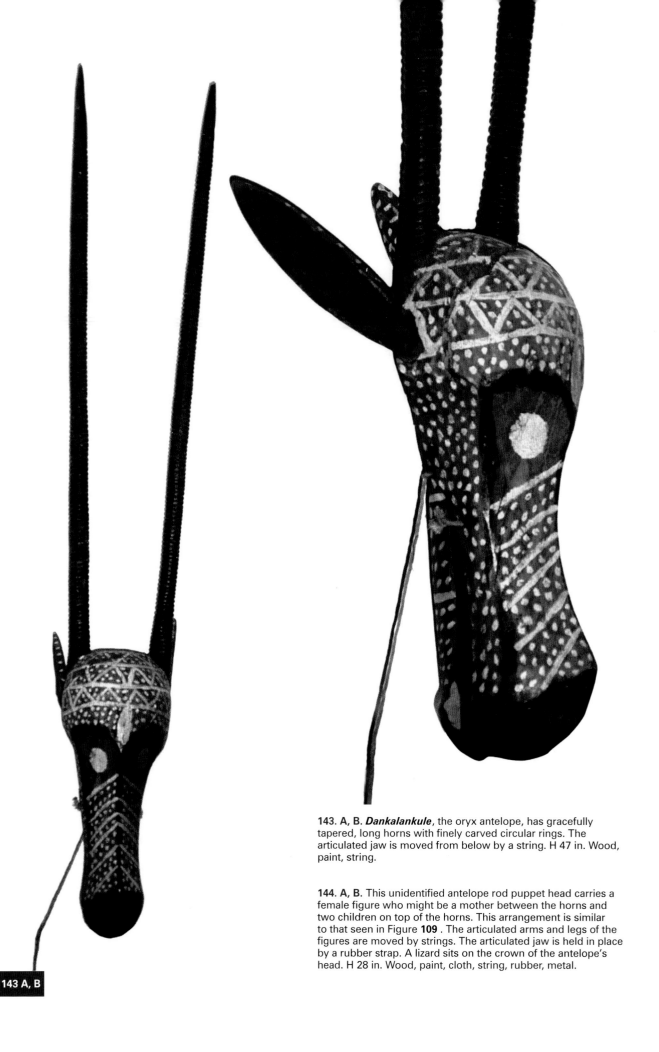

143. A, B. *Dankalankule*, the oryx antelope, has gracefully tapered, long horns with finely carved circular rings. The articulated jaw is moved from below by a string. H 47 in. Wood, paint, string.

144. A, B. This unidentified antelope rod puppet head carries a female figure who might be a mother between the horns and two children on top of the horns. This arrangement is similar to that seen in Figure **109** . The articulated arms and legs of the figures are moved by strings. The articulated jaw is held in place by a rubber strap. A lizard sits on the crown of the antelope's head. H 28 in. Wood, paint, cloth, string, rubber, metal.

143 A, B

145. Two sets of horns adorn this unusual rod puppet head of an unidentified antelope. See figures **56** and **60** for other antelope with multiple sets of horns. The articulated jaw, held in place by a rubber strap, is moved by a string from below. H 42.5 in. Wood, paint, rubber, metal, string.

146. **A, B.** The horns of this rod puppet head of an antelope support birds that may be ***Ngunaninje***, the cattle egret. Strings from below move the articulated limbs of the man with a black cap on the antelope's forehead. A string also moves the articulated jaw that is held in place by a rubber strap. H 25 in. Wood, paint, cloth, string, metal, rubber.

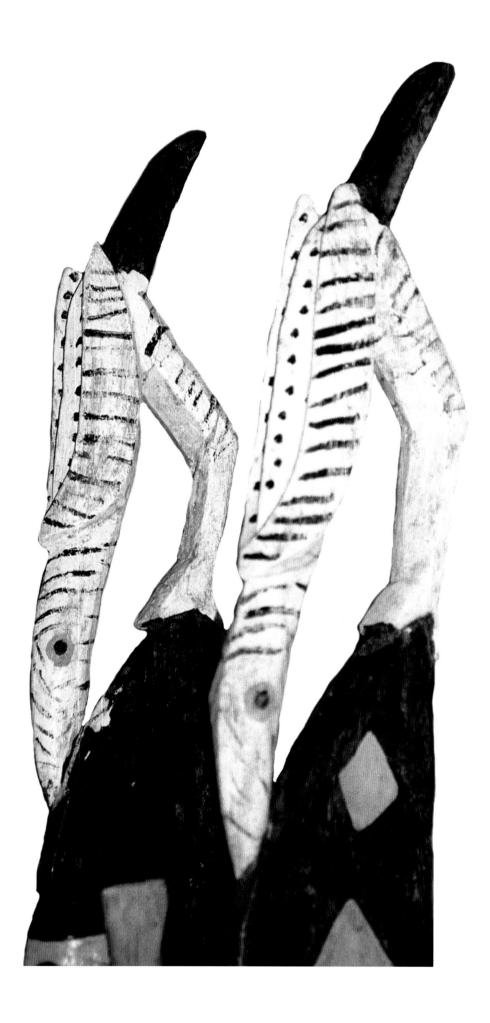

147. This animal rod puppet head has the horns and ears of an antelope and a dentate mouth suggestive of a carnivore. It is painted with the national colors of Mali: green, yellow, and red. The articulated jaw, held in place by a rubber strap, is moved from below by a string. H 34 in. Wood, paint, string, metal, cloth.

148. A, B. This animal rod puppet head has the horns and ears of an antelope and a sharply dentate mouth suggestive of a carnivore. The significance of "Parti du Mali" is unclear in this context. Literally translated as "Party of Mali", the phrase could refer to a political organization. In a phrase such as "prendre parti" the word "parti" can mean to choose or to be on the side of something, in this instance Mali. "Parti" could be a misspelling of or pun on the word "Patrie," meaning country or homeland. The articulated mouth is held in place by string. H 31.5 in. Wood, paint, string.

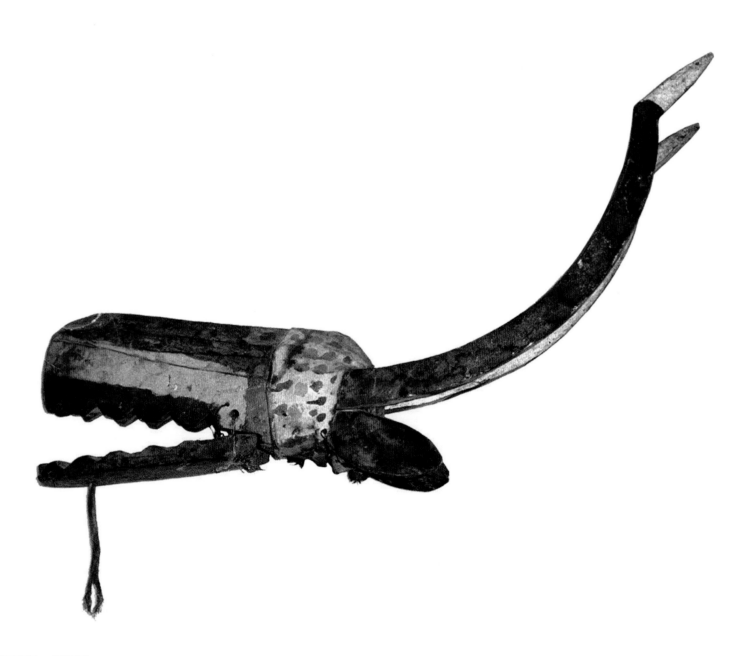

147

PARTI
DU
MALI

Kònòw, the birds, also play a significant role in the *Sogo bò* puppet theatre. Birds appear in performances organized by all ethnic groups. They serve as messengers for communication with the ancestors and with the world of spirits **(149, 150)**. Of particular importance among these shared characters is *Mali Kònò,* the Great Bird of Mali **(54,151-155)**. It celebrates Malian independence and is frequently decorated with the green, yellow and red colors of the national flag. This rod puppet head has features of the hornbill bird manifested by a long beak that curves slightly downward. A distinctive feature of the hornbill bird is a growth on the upper surface at the base of its beak that is said to contain the remains of its ancestors. On some rod puppet heads, carved fretwork referred to as a casque runs the length of the upper surface of *Mali Kònò's* beak where it represents the growth on the upper surface of the beak of a hornbill bird **(151, 152)**. In one example, the puppet is endowed with a painted replica of the fretwork and the hornbill's growth is represented by a prominence at the upper base of the beak **(155)**. A replica of an Islamic mosque finial **(151-153)**, an amulet **(155)** or a spiral crest **(154)** may be situated on the crown of *Mali Kònò's* head. The collection also includes rod puppets of *Dugon,* the hornbill bird **(156-159)**.

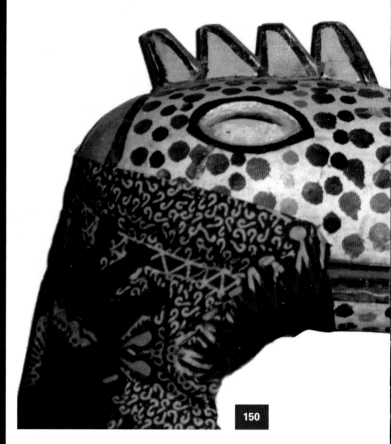

150

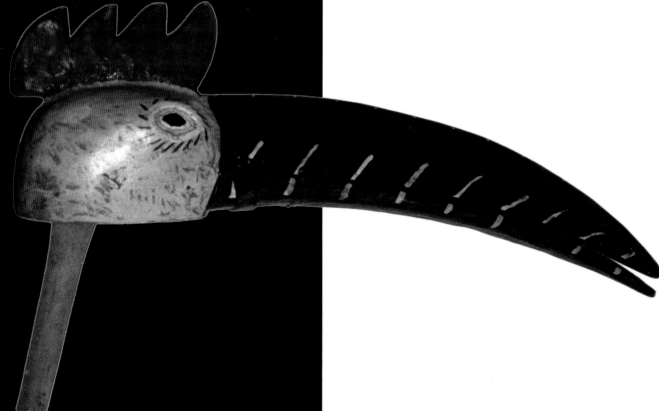

149

136

149. *Kònò*, the rod puppet head of a bird, may be a rooster. The articulated beak is supported by a rubber strap. H 9 in. Wood, paint, metal, rubber.

150. This rod puppet head of *Kònò*, a bird, may represent a rooster. It is decorated with linear arrays of multicolored dots on a white background. The sleeve over the handle is made of the same printed cotton cloth as the robe on the woman in Figure **87 B** and the sleeve of the ram puppet in Figure **105**. The beak is articulated with a rubber strap. H 7.5 in. Wood, paint, cloth, metal, rubber.

151. This rod puppet head of *Mali Kònò*, the Great Bird of Mali, has an elaborate crest with the Islamic crescent moon and star design that is found on mosque finials such as those illustrated in Figures **23** and **24**. The Malian national colors, green, yellow and red, are used in the fine, painted decoration. A casque on the upper beak is elaborate, carved fretwork. The articulated beak is supported by a rubber strap. H 25 in. Wood, paint, rubber, metal.

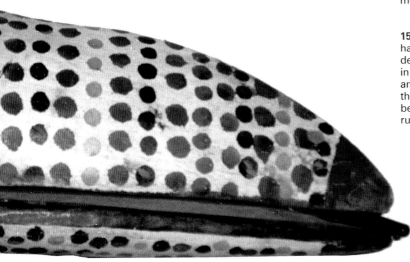

151

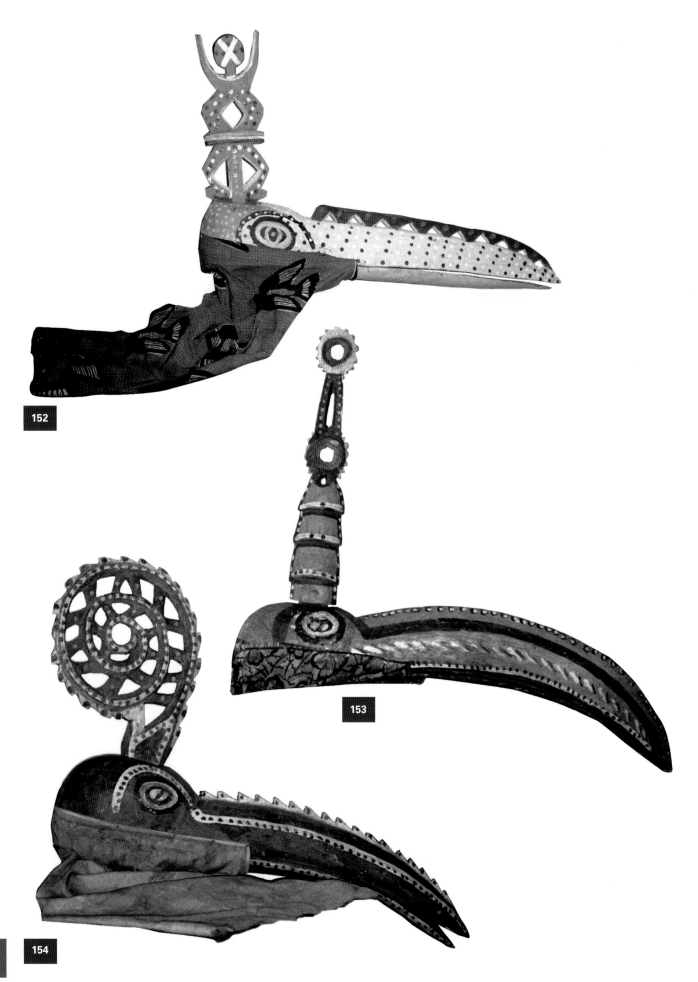

152

153

154

152. In this example, *Mali Kònò*, The Great Bird of Mali, has a crest with a disc and a crescent moon. These elements are also found on mosque finials such as the one illustrated in Figure **27.** The casque on *Mali Kònò's* beak consists of carved fretwork. Note the bird motif on the printed cotton cloth sleeve around the handle. The articulated beak is held in place by a rubber strap. H 26.5 in. Wood, paint, cloth, rubber, metal.

153. The crest on this rod puppet head of *Mali Kònò*, the Great Bird of Mali, suggests a mosque minaret with an open circle at the top of a finial as illustrated in Figures **25** and **26.** The casque on the beak consists of carved fretwork. Part of a printed cotton cloth sleeve is visible. A rubber strap supports the articulated beak. H 22 in. Wood, paint, cloth, metal.

154. This rod puppet head of *Mali Kònò*, the Great bird of Mali, has a carefully carved spiral crest on the crown of its head. A dentate casque has been carved on the upper surface of the beak. The sleeve of grey cloth matches the painted color of the bird's head. A rubber strap supports the articulated beak. H 21 in. Wood, paint, cloth, rubber, metal.

155. A, B. The crest of this rod puppet head of *Mali Kònò*, the Great Bird of Mali, suggests an amulet of the type that is used as a protective device. The white square on the side of *Mali Kònò's* head may also be a protective symbol. The prominence at the base of the beak refers to a similarly placed growth found on the beak of the hornbill bird. Rubber straps support the articulated beak. H 12 in. Wood, paint, rubber, string, metal.

155 A, B

139

156. This rod puppet head represents ***Dugon***, the hornbill bird. Note the prominence at the base of the beak. The articulated beak, supported by a rubber strap, is moved by a string. H 22 in. with rod. Wood, paint, metal, rubber, string.

157. A rod puppet head of ***Dugon***, the hornbill bird, with a heavy, hinged beak. Note the carved and painted motif along the upper part of the beak that resembles the casque on the beaks of ***Mali Kònò*** rod puppet heads in prior illustrations. H 9 in. Wood, paint, metal.

158. This rod puppet head of **Dugon**, the hornbill bird, has a long, slender articulated beak that is supported by a rubber strap. The crest is detachable. H 5 in. Wood, paint, rubber, metal.

159. This helmet mask probably represents ***Dugon***, the hornbill bird. H 15 in. Wood, paint.

Duga, the vulture (160), a bird that flies long distances in search of food is a metaphor for the hunter who must travel a great distance to find his prey. It symbolizes patience and perseverance.

In addition to performing some of the foregoing land animals in common with the Bamana people, the Boso enact a number of aquatic and amphibious animals. Fish may appear as body puppets or as freestanding objects, including some with articulated lateral fins (161-165). One of these is the dogfish or *Wulujègè,* a large fish noted for its sharp, serrated teeth that tear holes in fishermen's nets or cut their lines (70,164). The fisherman who catches a dogfish has accomplished a feat that is said to be comparable to the killing of a buffalo by a hunter. On the other hand, *Saalen,* the capitaine fish or Niger perch, is a mainstay of the fishermen's marketable catch and a staple food in the diet of the Boso people (28-30, 161). Free-standing objects such as these can be installed on the back of a *Sogo bò* puppet masquerade.

160. This mask that is worn on top of the head probably represents *Duga*, the vulture. Rings on its neck display the national colors of Mali. H 14.5 in. Wood, paint.

161. The Niger perch or *capitaine* fish, **Saalen**, is represented by this free-standing figure. Note the resemblance to *capitaine* fish in Figures **28, 29,** and **30.** H 6 in. Wood, paint.

162. This free-standing figure of an unidentified fish has articulated lateral fins held in place by rubber straps. H 6.5 in. Wood, paint, rubber, metal, string.

163. Articulated fins held in place by rubber straps on this unidentified free-standing fish are moved by strings. H 10 in. Wood, paint, rubber, metal, string.

164. This fish with prominent teeth is the dogfish, **Wulujègè**, in the form of a free-standing figure. The lateral fins are hinged and flap when the puppet is moved vigorously. H 8.5 in. Wood, paint, metal.

165. This colorful, unidentified free-standing fish has no articulated parts. It might be **Wulujègè**, the dogfish. H 10.5 in. Wood, paint.

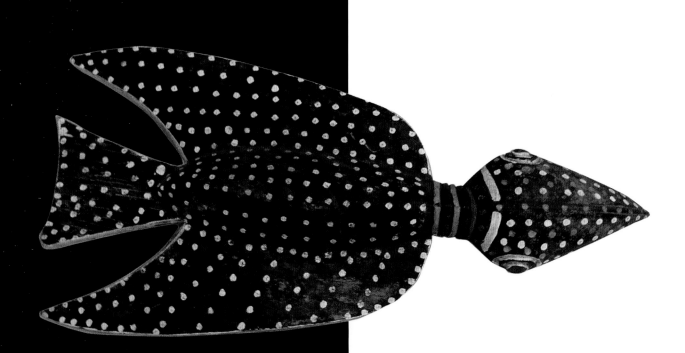

160

Mani, the hippopotamus, is a large aquatic animal that appears as a body puppet or as a rod puppet **(166)**. Although it is generally portrayed as a gentle creature, it can overturn a fisherman's boat. Performances usually refer to its small, soft eyes, its presence in the Niger River, and the affection with which the Boso people regard the hippopotamus.

Bama, the crocodile, may appear as an articulated puppet **(167-169)** or as a body puppet **(66)**. The crocodile represents impartial power, and it is said that a crocodile does not attack outside of its territory.

166. A, B. The rod puppet head of *Mani*, the hippopotamus, has a large, articulated mouth with prominent, white teeth. Part of a cloth sleeve covering the handle is evident. H 15 in. Wood, paint, cloth, metal.

167. The head, tail and legs of *Bama*, the crocodile, are articulated by cloth sleeves that connect these parts to the body. H 9 in. Wood, paint, cloth, metal.

168. The head, tail and legs of *Bama*, the crocodile, are articulated and connected to the body by cloth sleeves. H 18 in. Wood, paint, cloth, metal.

169 A, B. This 53-inch long, beautifully painted puppet depicts **Sama**, the crocodile, as it would appear when the animal is submerged with only its head visible above the water. The articulated jaw is held in place by a rubber strap. H 7.5 in. Wood, paint, rubber, metal.

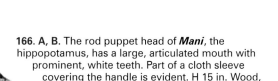

166 A, B

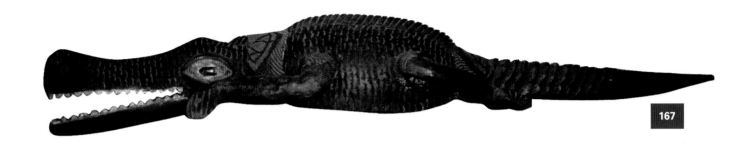

167

168

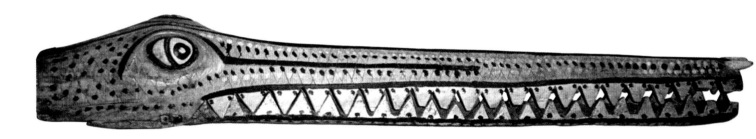

169 A, B

SPIRITS OF THE BUSH

Spirits of the water and bush are referred to as genies, a term derived from the Arabic word *jinn* (plural, *jinni*). *Jinni* are supernatural, invisible and shapeless. They may be present in inanimate objects as well as animals, and through these manifestations *Jinni* can exert good, evil or neutral influences on people or communities. The puppet collection includes several examples of bush spirit masks. They appear in daytime or nocturnal *Sogo bò* puppet performances of the Bamana and Boso as masked figures who are referred to as *Jinè* (62, 63, 170-172). *Wòkulòn* (173, 174) is one of the masked bush *Jinè*. Bush spirit masks are theriomorphic in that they have animal as well as human features. They participate in enactments of myths and legends that form part of *Sogo bò* puppet festivals.

170. A mask of *Jinè*, a bush spirit, with fearsome, predominantly animal features. H 20.5 in. Wood, paint, fiber, rubber, string, metal.

171. This mask of *Jinè*, a bush spirit, has human facial features and the horns of a goat or an antelope. H 19 in. Wood, paint, fiber.

172. A cap with horns sits on top of this mask of *Jinè*, a bush spirit with human facial features and transparent, glass eyes. A cowrie shell surrounded by beads is attached to the forehead, and there are painted facial scarifications. H 29.5 in. Wood, paint, horns, beads, cowrie shell, glass, cloth, metal.

170

146

173. This mask of **Wòkulòn**, a bush genie with bulbous eyes and large ears, has black and red spots painted on a yellow surface. H 13 in. Wood, paint.

174. This mask depicts **Wòkulòn**, a bush genie, with human and animal features. It has red and yellow spots painted on a grey surface. H 12 in. Wood, paint.

BEAUTIFUL WOMEN

Beautiful women appear in several guises as *Sogo bò* puppets (75, 175-181). *Mèrèn,* a marriageable woman or new bride (75, 175, 178, 180, 181), is identified by her *kunwililen* peaked coiffure that consists of hair braided across the crown from ear to ear, ending in a dependant curl or braid on either side. She appears as a body puppet or rod puppet.

Yayaroba (5-7, 44, 46, 176) is a more recent incarnation of the ideal, beautiful woman of high moral standards who cannot be ignored. She appears as a rod or bust body puppet with a very ample bosom who wears the *ko taa* hairstyle composed of braids in rows from the forehead to the back of the head. She sometimes performs with a jealous husband who guards her with a sword or a rod (44, 45). *Yayaroba's* large, prominent breasts, full coiffure, and healthy appearance represent prosperity, abundance, and a harmonious home. She moves slowly around the performance area, turning her head from side to side and moving her arms up and down to the accompaniment of a song that praises her beauty, health, and outstanding moral character.

175

175. This puppet figure of a beautiful woman has arms articulated at the elbows and shoulders. Her jewelry consists of painted neck rings and earrings with beads. The palms of her hands are painted to display henna decorations that are worn on important occasions. The traditional *kunwililen* hairstyle may identify her as a young bride. The block base was probably attached to an armature placed over the performer's head. Unpainted parts of the puppet were covered with a cloth robe with apertures for the protruding breasts. H 33 in. Wood, paint, metal, beads.

176. The *ko taa* hairstyle consisting of braids running from the front to the back of the head adorns this female figure who is probably **Yayaroba**. There is a painted indigo tattoo below her lower lip. The serrated, two-legged base was probably installed in an armature that was placed over the performer's head. A cloth robe with apertures for the protruding breasts would cover the unpainted areas. She has no articulated parts. H 30 in. Wood, paint.

177. This beautiful female figure may be **Yayaroba**. She has painted scarifications on her forehead and cheeks. Glass discs cover her painted eyes. The jug-handle "arms" and painted, cup-shaped base were probably used to attach the puppet in some fashion above the performer's head. The fact that the torso, arms and base were painted suggests that they may have been exposed. She has no articulated parts. H 26.5 in. Wood, paint, glass.

178. This beautiful female figure has an unusually flat contour. The traditional *kunwililen* hairstyle suggests that she may be a young bride. Painted designs on her hands represent henna decorations that are worn on important occasions. The arms are articulated at the shoulders and elbows. Unpainted areas were covered with cloth, including the upper arms, with apertures for the protruding breasts. The flat peg at the base was probably placed in an armature. H 17 in. Wood, paint, metal.

179. The cotton print robe worn by this tall rod puppet figure of a beautiful woman covers strings that move her articulated arms. The appended, protruding bosom made of cloth is an unusual feature of this puppet. H 44 in. Wood, paint, cloth, metal, string.

180. This habitable rod puppet figure of a beautiful woman wears the *kunwililen* hairstyle. Articulated at the shoulders, her arms are moved by sticks. She wears a robe made of printed cotton cloth. This puppet was obtained from Yaya Coulibaly in 2003. H 39 in. Wood, cloth, paint.

181. This body puppet of a beautiful woman wears the *kunwililen* hairstyle. The base would probably have been inserted into a cloth-covered armature that would be placed over the performer, leaving the puppet's bosom exposed. H 39 in. Wood, paint.

179

180

181

Jobali appears as a mask. She is a beautiful woman who is vain and unwilling to marry **(182)**.

Faro is a beautiful female genie who lives in the water **(183-186)**. She appears as a rod puppet, sometimes in the form of a mermaid with articulated arms. Her allure and beauty are a two edged metaphor for the life of the Boso people that is intimately tied to the Niger River. On the one hand, *Faro*, the spirit of the water, represents the potential for an abundant harvest of fish and other aquatic animals needed to sustain the Boso community. On the other hand, *Faro* is a manifestation of the unpredictability of fishing and perils fishermen face on the water because it is said that her beauty is so dangerous that men who see her face are destined to die.

182

182. **Jobali**, the vain, beautiful woman, is represented by this mask. She and the four female figures on her head wear the *kunwililen* hairstyle. The four female figures might be a metaphor for the vanity of a woman who is consumed with an exaggerated impression of her beauty. H 22 in. Wood, paint, rubber, metal.

183. **A, B.** This figure of **Faro**, the water genie, is outfitted with an elaborate, painted robe that covers most of her truncated arms and body, with an opening at the bottom to expose her forked tail. A knob visible at the bottom of the puppet opposite the tail is the remainder of a rod that was used to hold this object. Her long, flowing hair is visible in the back. This puppet has no articulated parts. H 40 in. Wood, paint.

183 A, B

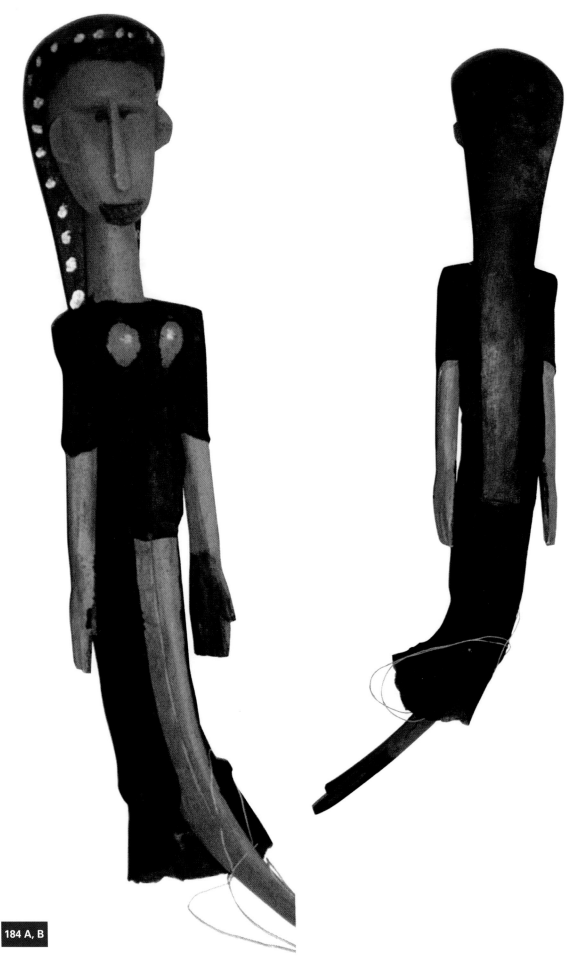

184 A, B

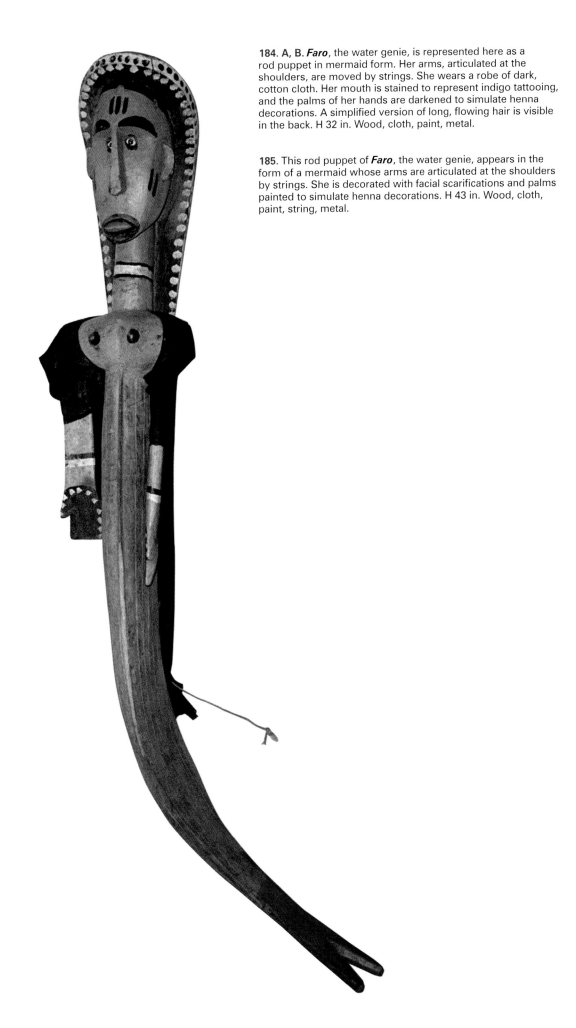

184. A, B. *Faro*, the water genie, is represented here as a rod puppet in mermaid form. Her arms, articulated at the shoulders, are moved by strings. She wears a robe of dark, cotton cloth. Her mouth is stained to represent indigo tattooing, and the palms of her hands are darkened to simulate henna decorations. A simplified version of long, flowing hair is visible in the back. H 32 in. Wood, cloth, paint, metal.

185. This rod puppet of ***Faro***, the water genie, appears in the form of a mermaid whose arms are articulated at the shoulders by strings. She is decorated with facial scarifications and palms painted to simulate henna decorations. H 43 in. Wood, cloth, paint, string, metal.

185

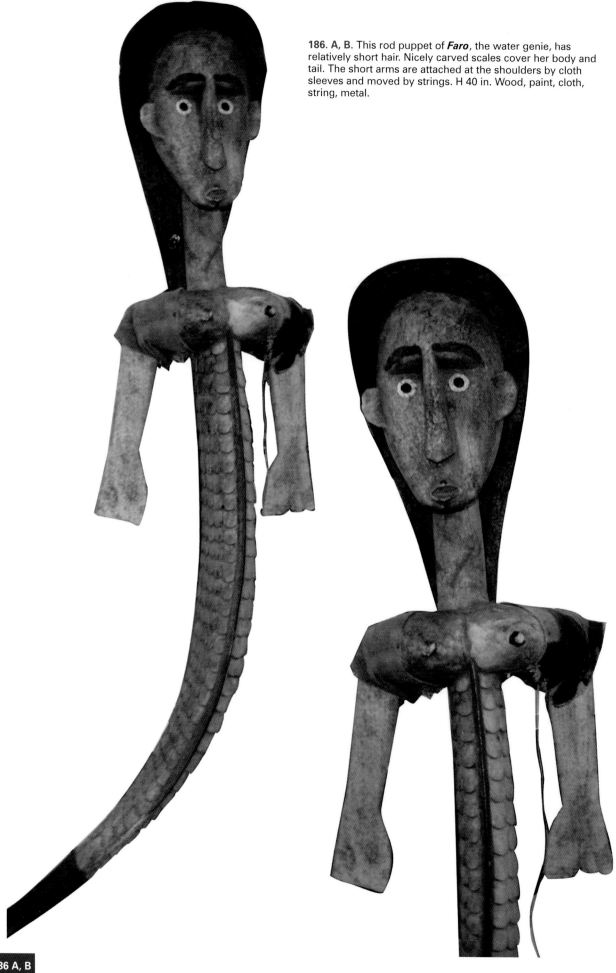

186. A, B. This rod puppet of *Faro*, the water genie, has relatively short hair. Nicely carved scales cover her body and tail. The short arms are attached at the shoulders by cloth sleeves and moved by strings. H 40 in. Wood, paint, cloth, string, metal.

186 A, B

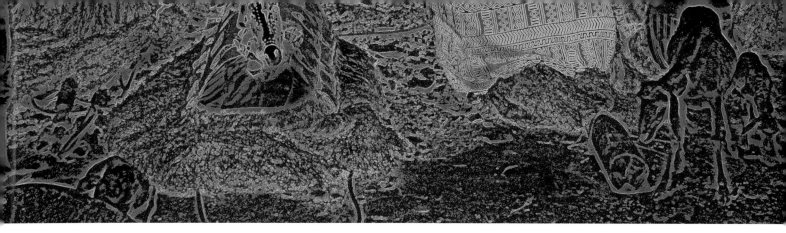

COLOR AND OTHER EMBELLISHMENTS

As illustrated in this book, vibrant colors play an important role in the contemporary performance of *Sogo bò* masks, puppets, and puppet masquerades. The colors are chosen to enhance the beauty and attractiveness of the puppets and masks, to increase their visibility, and to heighten the dramatic effect of the entire performance. Bright, commercial enamel paints, as well as various textiles used to cover the puppets and masquerades, greatly enliven the show. The frequent use of green, yellow, and red is a reference to the national colors of Mali.

In addition to "sweetening" the appearance of the puppet or mask, a color might also be chosen as the sign of a particular meaning attached to the performance object. It is remarkable that similar significance is sometimes associated with a particular color or combination of colors in widely disparate cultures throughout Africa.

White, the absence of color, is an attribute of the ancestors. It denotes positive qualities such as peace, divinity, tranquility, goodwill, and wisdom but sometimes also illness and misfortune. Sources of white used by various African cultures, other than commercial paints, include facial makeup powder, dried clay or kaolin, talcum powder, and dental powder.

Black denotes sorcery, death, and disturbance. It can also indicate mental imbalance. The most common non-commercial source of black pigment is a mixture of soot or powdered charcoal with oil. Other black pigments include shoe polish, ink from pens, and commercial paint.

Blue is associated with death but also with water and the sky. Before the ready availability of commercial paints, the most common source of blue pigment was indigo dye extracted from the *indigofera* plant. Another traditional source sometimes still in use is laundry bluing compound in which indigo is usually the pigment. Today, synthetic indigo is produced commercially.

Red indicates certain emotional qualities, magical power, physical strength and courage as well as irresistible sexual attraction and purity. It is appropriate for a hunter or a warrior. Traditional sources of red pigment were ground plant or mineral materials.

Yellow and **ochre** are colors associated with life and joy. In addition to commercial paints, yellow and ochre are obtained from plant and mineral materials. An important source of these colors in some areas is clay.

Red and white together denote the reunion of the living and the dead. In some initiation ceremonies, the initiate's body is covered with red pigment and spotted with white dots.

Appliqued metal sheets of brass or aluminum with embossed designs and metal strips are also used to energize sculptures and masks, especially in nocturnal performances.

Small **mirrors or glass** inserts in puppets' eyes are thought to be endowed with mystical power that is manifested by the glowing light reflected from at night.

Female puppets often wear **jewelry**, such as earrings made from beads and cowrie shells.

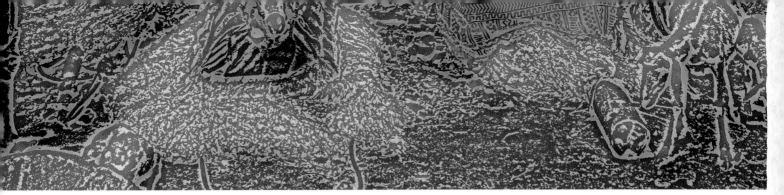

BIBLIOGRAPHY

Arnoldi, MJ. *Playing with Time. Art and Performance in Central Mali.* Bloomington, Indiana: Indiana University Press,1995.

Arnoldi, MJ. J-P Colleyn (Ed). "The *Sogow*: Imagining a Moral Universe Through *Sogo bò* Masquerades." *Bamana. The Art of Existence in Mali*. New York, New York: The Museum for African Art, 2001.

Blumenthal, E. *Puppetry: A World History*. New York, New York: Harry N Abrams, 2005.

Bodson, L. *Yaya Coulibaly: Marionnettiste*. Bamako, Mali: Edition de L'Oeil, 2002.

Clapperton, H. *Journal of the Second Expedition into the Interior of Africa*. Philadelphia, Pennsylvania: Carey, Lea & Carey, 1829.

Colleyn, J-P. *Bamana. Visions of Africa.* Milan, Italy: 5 Continents Editions, 2009.

Dagan, EA. *Emotions in Motion/La Magie de L'Imaginaire.* Montreal, Canada: Galerie Amrad, 1990.

Darkowska-Nidzgorski, O. and Nidzgorski, D. *Marionnettes et Masques au Coeur du Theatre Africain.* SEPIA. Saint-Maur, France: Institut International de la Marionette,1998.

Davis, C. B. *The Animal Motif in Bamana Art*. New Orleans, Louisiana: The Davis Gallery, 1981.

den Otter, E. "Of Masks and Men: Visible and Hidden Dancers of the Bamana and Bozo (Mali)." *The Spirits Dance in Africa. Evolution, Transformation and Continuity in Sub-Sahara.* EA Dagan (Ed). Montreal, Canada: Galerie Amrad, 1997.

den Otter, E. and Kéïta, M. *Sogo Bo. La fete des masques bamanan*. Bamako, Mali: Imprime Color, 2002.

Favreau, A. "Masques et Marionnettes du Mali," *Marionnettes du Mali. Masques et Marionnettes du Thèâtre Sogobò*. R. Groux, (Ed). Montreuil-Sous-Bois, France: Au Fil du Fleuve, 2005.

Herreman F. *To Cure and Protect: Sickness and Health in African Art*. New York, New York: The Museum for African Art, 1999.

Kruger, M. "The power of double vision: tradition and social intervention in African puppet performance." *NTQ* 22:324-335, 2006.

Ibn Battuta. *Travels in Asia and Africa, 1325-1354*. Translated by HAR Gibb. London, England: George Routledge & Sons, 1929.

Imperato, P. J. "Bambara and Malinke ton masquerades." *African Arts* 13(4): 47-55,82-85, 87, 1980.

Imperato, P. J. "The Yayaroba puppet tradition in Mali." *Puppetry J* 32(4):20-26, 1981.

Imperato, P. J. "The depiction of beautiful women in Malian youth association masquerades," *African Arts* 27(1): 58-65,95-96, 1994.

Jacobson-Widding, A. "Red-White-Black as a Mode of Thought. A Study of Triadic Classification by Colours in the Ritual Symbolism and Cognitive Thought of the Peoples of the Lower Congo." *Acta Universitatis Upsaliensis, Uppsala Studies in Cultural Anthropology #1*, 1979, pp. 168-171.

Jones, B. "The Magical Life of Objects: An Interview with Adrian Kohler and Basil Jones." *Lincoln Center Theater Review*. 55 (Spring): 10-14, 2011.

Ndiaye, F. and Massa, G. *L'Oiseau dans l'Art de l'Afrique de l'Ouest.* Paris, France: Editions Sepia, Societe des Amateurs de l'Art Africain, 2004.

Reeder, R. "Puppets: Moving Sculpture." *J Decorative and Propaganda Arts* 11 (Winter):106-121, 1989.

Siegmann, W. C. "Spirits, Men and Masks," *Assuming the Guise. African Masks Considered and Reconsidered.* Williamstown, Massachusetts: Williams College Museum of Art, 1991.

Soleillet, P. *Voyages et Decouvertes de Paul Soleillet.* Paris, France: Gros, 1886.

Werewere-Liking. *Statuettes Peintes d'Afrique de l'Ouest. Marionnettes du Mali.* Paris, France: ARHIS, 1987.

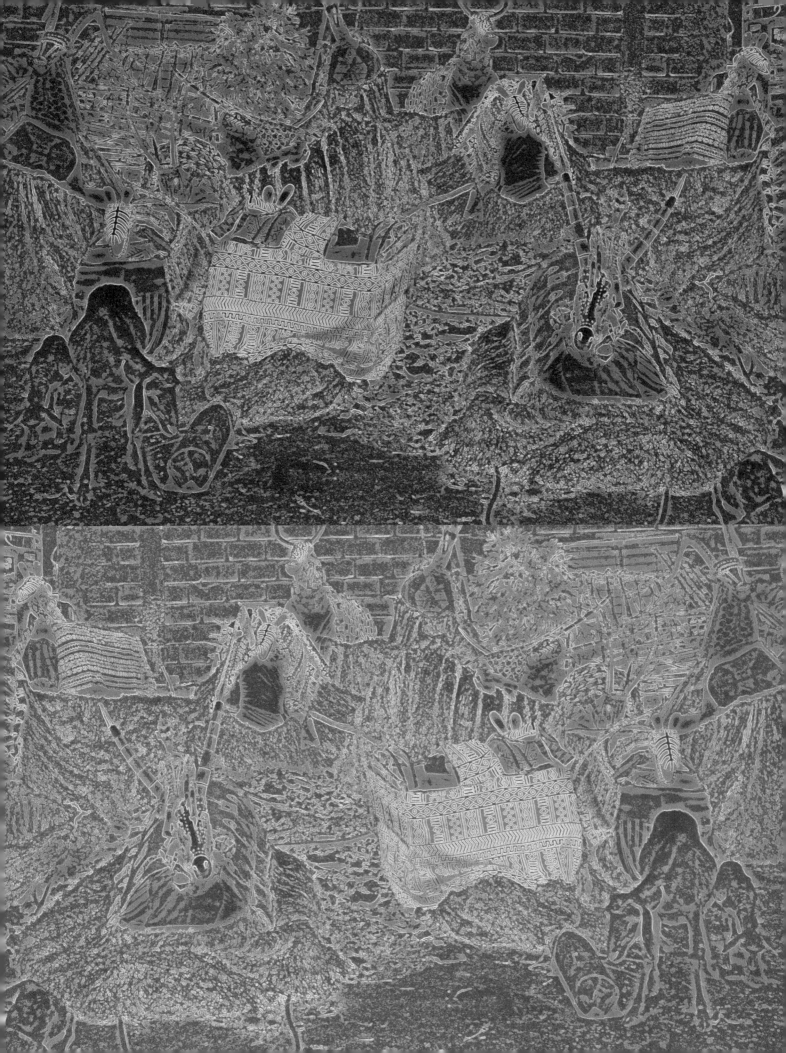